Bon Vo[yage]

'I'll get this old crate airborne if it's the last thing I do.'
—*Kidnapper of Nigerian diplomat Mr Umaru Dikko*

'Chocs away!'
—*Sir Adrian Cadbury*

'Clear the runway – I'm coming in.'
—*Cyril Smith MP*

Perhaps you best not read this on the 'plane!

Plane Crazy

Graham Jones

ARROW BOOKS

Arrow Books Limited
62–65 Chandos Place, London WC2N 4NW

An imprint of Century Hutchinson Ltd

London Melbourne Sydney Auckland
Johannesburg and agencies throughout
the world

First published by Arrow 1986

Printed and bound in Great Britain by
Anchor Brendon Limited, Tiptree, Essex

ISBN 0 09 946250 8

This book is dedicated to my mother,
who must like flying as she's always
jetting off somewhere.

Check In Here, Please

Grateful Thanks ...

Firstly, I should like to thank Anthony Cheetham whose (brilliant!) idea this book was.

Second, sincere thanks to the following who turned a marvellous idea into something special: The Rt Hon. Norman Tebbit PC, MP; The Rt Hon. David Steel PC, MP; Kingsley Amis CBE; Eamonn Andrews CBE; Christopher Biggins; Lord Bottomley of Cleveland OBE, PC; Art Buchwald; Barbara Cartland; Sir Jeremy Child; Les Dawson; Sandor Elès; Sir Ranulph Fiennes; Dick Francis OBE; Lord Grade of Elstree Kt; Michael Grade; Dr Germaine Greer; General Alexander M. Haig, jnr.; Gorden Kaye; Roy Kinnear; Robin Knox-Johnston CBE; Rula Lenska; Christopher Martin-Jenkins; Barry Norman, Jon Pertwee; Steve Race; Anneka Rice; Diana Rigg; Brian Rix CBE; Brough Scott; Mike Smith; Julie Walters; Dave Wetzel; Captain Geoffrey Whittaker; Ernie Wise OBE; Britannia Airways; Cathay Pacific Airlines; Orion Airways; Pan American Airways.

Thirdly, heartfelt gratitude to the friends who willingly contributed anecdotes, rude or otherwise.

Fourthly, thanks to the authors of the small handful of works which actually touched on the humorous side of flying – they will find themselves listed in the course of the book. Also thanks to Methuen, London, for permission to reproduce extracts from *Lillee, Over and Out* by Dennis Lillee, and to Sphere Books for permission to reproduce extracts from *The Stewardesses* by Penny Sutton.

And finally, thanks to my wife Lynne who did much of the hard work.

Please Fasten Your Seatbelts

I approached the stewardess manfully, and whispered seductively in her ear. 'You'll never believe this,' I said, 'but I'm writing a book on the funniest things to happen to people during air journeys. I wondered whether you'd be able to help.'

Through icy blue eyes she gave me a stern, obviously practised look – half headmistress, half gorilla, as if I'd just rifled the float from the duty-free trolley or done something unmentionable with my stereo headphones.

'No, I don't believe you,' she replied, cold as a midnight stacking over Stavanger. 'If you're trying to chat me up you'll have to do a darn sight better than that.'

This, you will realize, has not been an easy book to research. I discovered later that 'I am writing a book about all the funny things to happen to people during air journeys', is the third most common chat-up line used on stewardesses by would be mile-high romeos, and is specifically warned of at training school.

I was hurt, though not so much by the fact that she didn't believe me. Since, as far as I know, this is the first work of its type ever to appear, what was really upsetting was knowing that hundreds of lucky males had been for three generations swinging from hotel-room chandeliers, creeping with their conquests to secret compartments in the rear of airliners, or at least getting an extra Scotch and ginger – all on credit for my book.

Still, they'll have to believe me now, though I am expecting a few coffees in my lap, not to mention stale bread-rolls in my coffee, after revelations like THE WORLD'S STEAMIEST AIR GIRLS and A DOZEN WAYS STEWARDESSES GET REVENGE ON PASSENGERS THEY TAKE A DISLIKE TO. ('Here, Mr Jones, this will no doubt help with your next book – splosh!')

That goes for those knights of the skyways, pilots, too. I can see that in future I will have to check in under a false name. 'This is your Captain speaking, I'm sorry but we've got Graham Jones aboard, and after reading his last book we will just have to make a short stopover in Frankfurt so we can nail him into a crate and send him back airfreight.'

Well, I hope they will read *Plane Crazy* anyway, even if it is deliberately non-technical and aimed at the everyday passenger like you or me, or Joan Collins, or Richard Harris – anyone that is, who is less concerned about landing air speeds and visual slope display indicators than the really important things in flying like how soon you will get your first meal and how the duty-free prices compare with Zurich.

In preparing this sensational, gripping and, if I may say so, devastatingly amusing work, I have been greatly assisted by a host of much-travelled celebrities, all of whom I am glad to say share the crucial preoccupations of the rest of us, e.g., how good-looking the stewardesses (or stewards) are . . . will they be nice to us . . . if we get a second cup of coffee, will the cream and sugar run out (no, on second thoughts, that's a foregone conclusion) . . . what can we do for eight and a half hours to avoid conversation with the most boring person in the world who for some unlucky reason is always large, lacking in deodorant, and plonked in the adjacent seat?

No, don't take me too seriously. Flying is a delight, a thrill; along with caviar, champagne, romance and duty-free gin, it is one of life's great pleasures. Yes, on one or two airlines you might even be able to combine the lot. (OK, well maybe not on Aeroflot.)

When I began this book, friends suggested I was a little deranged. I must have been suffering from lack of oxygen to the brain. Too much high-altitude travel. After all, what at all amusing is there to tell about air journeys? You'll be surprised, I said . . . and I was surprised too. For trawling the flying community for contributions has provided one of the richest crops of amusing, bizarre, and downright crazy tales.

You don't believe me? Well, may I suggest you fasten your seatbelts (no need to extinguish cigarettes or wink at the stewardess – Ed.) sit right back, and come fly with us . . .

Aeroplanes, Airlines, Airports

No, I have not been hijacked to Honolulu (though I live in hope), been bitten by an anaconda popping up out of the duty-frees, tried to sleepwalk out of the emergency exit at 35,000 feet, or suffered a heart attack after making mad passionate love to three stewardesses in the mink-lined tail section of a DC–8.

That is not to say every air journey I have been on has been uneventful. Only up to a point. My second most interesting moment came while travelling on MEA to Beirut (yes, I agree it was a funny place to choose for a holiday) when the plane was delayed for half an hour. Why? I asked the purser. 'Oh, nothing,' he shrugged. 'It's just that they've arrested two of the passengers for trying to bring guns on board.' Well, the system worked, I reckoned. Hard luck, though, no hijack to Hawaii – not this trip at least.

Undoubtedly my most bizarre moment came when I was detained at Heathrow as a suspected hijacker. The X-ray scanner showed up a *pair of scissors* in my hand baggage and I was immediately hustled to one side as a suspected Carlos. I could, of course, just see myself rushing to the cockpit: 'Change course to Cuba, Captain, or I'll cut off your gold armbands, one by one.'

So, welcome to that strange, heady and wonderful

14

Plane Crazy world of sumptuous fare, delectable duty-frees, beautiful stewardesses, lovable fellow passengers, smash-hit in-flight movies – where absolutely *anything* can (and does!) happen . . .

Most unusual flight delay

In December 1969 ninety-five passengers on a BEA Trident jet to Geneva were waiting to board when loader Norman Penn raised a hand and the other loaders scattered in all directions.

Coming from one of the suitcases was a buzzing sound. Someone shouted, 'It's a bomb.' A loudspeaker request was made for all passengers to collect their luggage, and every item was claimed except a small light-grey overnight case.

The offending baggage was carried to a remote part of the airport and a bomb-disposal unit moved in as firemen stood by. The case was opened very, very carefully and inside was found . . . frilly underwear, stockings, make-up, and a battery hand-held personal object, switched on.

The owner was by this time safely vibrating her way to Geneva, and BEA did not wish to embarrass her by naming her. 'Obviously she was a foreigner or she would have understood the loudspeaker appeal,' said a spokesman.

Nastiest nip in the air

There can be few less comfortable places for a gentleman to have an accident with his trouser zip than 38,000 feet above the Atlantic. Yet this is what happened to an unfortunate high-flying American in March 1976 on a TWA flight from Los Angeles to London. The passenger was in the lavatory when

excruciating pain struck. He rang for the stewardess. She nearly fainted at the sight. The steward was called. He didn't faint, but, powerless to separate zipper from male anatomy, called the pilot. Luckily, the pilot didn't faint either. Instead he radioed Heathrow for a doctor to stand by. When the plane did touch down relief was at hand. Man and fly were separated with the aid of tweezers, pliers (ouch!), olive oil, local anaesthetic ... and what airline officials called 'a quick tug' (ouch! again). The incident was not entered in the plane's log. Said the doctor: 'I know the Latin for the object, but not the ailment.'

World's most unusual boarding procedure

Well, it was democratic, to a point anyway. Hugh Williams, a twenty-seven-year-old marketing executive with a soft drinks firm told the magazine *Executive Travel* in September 1985 of the novel procedure for gaining a seat on a flight from Port Harcourt in Nigeria to the capital, Lagos. After two planes failed to materialize, it became obvious that there would be three times the number of passengers for the third flight as the number of seats. Then the army took over and imposed a quite logical solution: all the passengers should run twice around the plane and back. The fastest would win boarding passes. Mr Williams and some European business colleagues must all either have been desperate or had wings on their heels. They were all comfortably among the first to finish.

Norman Tebbit

Cabinet Minister, and Britain's most famous and influential ex-pilot, Chairman of the Conservative Party

So many of my fondest memories of my flying days are either too technical to be understood by the layman or too vulgar to be printed over my name! However, a couple of fond memories which may raise a chuckle.

Memory No. 1
Many years ago when I was flying DC7s (they had propellers!) across the Atlantic a really unpleasant lady passenger returning from America to live in London was throughout the journey rude, demanding, arrogant and plain nasty. Naturally – as it was BOAC – our cabin staff treated her politely and well. However, as we approached London she called for the stewardess once again. 'What,' she demanded, 'is the position concerning domestic staff, housemaids and all that in London?'

'Are you a British citizen, madam?' asked the stewardess.

'Yes,' came the reply.

'Then,' said the stewardess with ill-concealed icy rage, 'you should have no difficulty obtaining a post provided you behave in a civil manner to your employer.'

Memory No. 2

My favourite personal recollection is of sitting on the flight-deck of a 707 awaiting take-off from New York on an absolutely filthy day. It was some years ago when the now-defunct Braniff airline had broken away from the convention of more or less plain white or silver-coloured aircraft and begun painting theirs in the most hideous sludge-brown and green colours.

A voice came over the radio:

'Hey, Braniff – what did you fly through?'

Most unfortunate stopover hotel booking

In June 1982 a vicar received an apology after British Caledonian Airways booked him overnight into a Hong Kong brothel. The airline had agreed to put up 220 passengers stranded when a DC-10 flight to Gatwick was held up by a mechanical fault. Unfortunately the delay coincided with a Chinese festival, and all the airline's listed hotels in Hong Kong were full. As a result, the unsuspecting priest found himself in a room with a circular bed, walls lined with mirrors, and a resident 'lady in waiting'.

A B.Cal. spokesman said: 'The flight was delayed for two days. Unfortunately on the second night the vicar found himself in a place which was obviously tailored for people with somewhat more exotic tastes. But he was not approached by any lady member of the staff. We have sent him a letter explaining our difficulties and how the problem arose, and hope it will be accepted.'

Most sumptuous airline meal

Leading nomination for this is Cathay Pacific's 'Gourmet Air Express' in June 1985, when eighty invited guests took part in a literally moveable feast 35,000 feet over the Pacific, as a gleaming new Boeing 747–300 was delivered from Vancouver to Cathay Pacific's headquarters in Hong Kong. The meal was prepared by three chefs from London's Dorchester Hotel, led by renowned Maître Chef de Cuisine Anton Mossiman with the airline's own chef de cuisine, Gebhard Scherrer. There were two meals. The menus and wine lists were as follows:

LUNCHEON

Parfait de foie de volaille Dorchester
A fine chicken liver terrine with truffles

Goutte d'or en surprise
Clear consommé with puff-pastry case

Rendez-vous de poissons grillés
Combination of grilled fish

Granité au Champagne
Granité with Champagne

Filet de boeuf mariné
Fillet of beef with almond oil and herbs

Salade d'asperges
Asparagus salad

Fromages
Selection of cheeses

Trois mousses de fruits de la saison
Three fruit mousses with mango sauce

Café ou thé Chinoise

Chocolats

THE WINES

Cristal L. Roederer 1979 Champagne

Batard-Montrachet 1982, J. Drouhin

Cristal L. Roederer 1979 Champagne

Bonnes-Mares 1979, Nuits-St Georges, Moillard

Château l'Angélus 1975, St Emilion

Château d'Yquem 1980

Liqueurs

DINNER

Gaspacho moderne
A light, chilled fresh vegetable soup

Mignon de veau en croute
Delicate fillet of veal with a light herb sauce

Steak de saumon poché aux petits légumes
Poached salmon steak with choice vegetables

Fromages
International cheese board

Terrine d'oranges à la menthe
Orange terrine flavoured with mint and served with
raspberry sauce

Café ou thé Chinoise

Chocolats

THE WINES

Cristal L. Roederer 1979 Champagne

Echezeaux 1978, Le Roy

Chablis Grand Cru Les Clos 1983, Henri Laroche

Château Batailley 1970, Pauillac

Château d'Yquem 1980

Armagnac 1914

Cognac Rémy Martin Louis XIII

Liqueurs

After the flight Mr Scherrer said that Cathay would
be trying to match the standards on their flights
with *cuisine naturelle:* 'We want to make eating in
the air as exciting as aviation itself,' he enthused.

The celebrities' favourite airline

Lord (Lew) Grade prefers BA. 'I have always endeavoured to use British Airways because I feel it is important to support our own airline.' So does Diana Rigg: 'Personnel speak my language.' And with those casting votes in my quick straw-poll of celebrities contributing to this book, British Airways can certainly claim to be the high-flyers' favourite.

A senior European politician I spoke to was among those with a slightly different choice, Singapore Airlines, which emerged a clear second.

Tying for third place were TWA and Air New Zealand. *Plane Crazy*'s high-flyers were a bit more reticent at nominating the airlines they didn't like. But the three mentioned most often for the in-flight plastic spoon were Air Maroc, Qantas and Sabena (see David Steel, p 102 for a novel translation of the title of the latter!).

Meanwhile a wholly unsolicited testimonial as to why British Airways is the celebrities' favourite comes from John Coghlan, who beat his way to fame as the drummer with the rock group Status Quo.

Mr Coghlan told the *Star* in January 1986 that BA were tops for (dare we say it?) SEX. His version of how the airline takes good care of you:

'I owe my membership of the Mile High Club to a British Airways hostess. Most of the rest of the band do as well. And the BA girls would regularly 'renew' our membership of the club.

'There has been many a time that we've arrived in a strange place and it's BA girls who have helped us get over the jet-lag in the nicest possible way.'

He went on to brag: 'More than once I've had a couple of BA hostesses at a time. Sometimes they would deliberately wear their uniforms at parties for us, with stockings and suspenders underneath. I've tried other airlines but my vote was always for British Airways.

'Whenever we boarded a BA plane for a long flight we used to wonder what was going to happen!'

No, in case you are wondering, this is *not* Lord Grade's experience. He told me, 'I am afraid I am never involved in any strange or bizarre incidents when I travel by air.'

Favourite airline nicknames

Every airline has a pet name among the in-crowd of flight deck and cabin crew. Among the best, past and present are:

BEA	Back Every Afternoon
BOAC	Better on a Camel
	Bend Over Again Christine
CP Air	Can't Promise Anything
Air France	Air Chance
Iberia	Hysteria
LIAT	Luggage in Any Town
Pan Am	Pandemonium Scareways
Qantas	Queer and Nice Types of Stewards
SAS	Sweet and Sexy
SASHA	Stay at Home, Stay Alive
TWA	Try Walking Airlines

World's least favourite airline

Getting the strongest backing for this accolade after the summer of 1985 was the Rumanian state airline Tarom. Scores of passengers on charter flights to

24

Black Sea resorts wrote to newspapers and TV travel programmes protesting at the 'missing' safety drills, poor provision of food, a 'primitive' drinks trolley, coffee served without milk or sugar, and off-hand and discourteous service.

Wrote one holidaymaker: 'The cabin staff spent the entire flight behind closed curtains smoking and drinking.' Wrote another: 'The worst airline I have travelled on. Not enough drinks for everyone, and shabby toilets with no toilet roll.' One sunseeker got trapped in the lavatory because there was no knob on the inside, though the favourite story told to me was by the holidaymaker who said that during take-off he had to keep his foot on the carpet in the aisle because it kept trying to roll itself up as the plane climbed skyward.

World's most religious airline

This title was grabbed from more established rivals in December 1985 with the debut of 'The Lord's Airline', flying pilgrims from Miami to Tel Aviv via Luxembourg for a round trip fare of $1000. The ageing DC–8 purchased from Air Canada was baptized as 'The Spirit of Jerusalem' by a rabbi using water from the Jordan river; it boasted murals depicting the city of Jerusalem and the Ten Commandments written in English and Hebrew.

The Lord's Airline was the brainchild of A. Ari Marshall, a Turkish born-again Christian, whose credentials included a spell working for the Soviet airline Aeroflot. In-flight service included free bibles and miniature Torahs, but no alcohol.

Said Mr Marshall: 'The Israelis have their own airline, the Arabs have their own airline. Why shouldn't the Lord have an airline?'

Art Buchwald

US humorist

Craziest journey

The US airlines have been promoting all sorts of special fares lately and it's very bewildering when you're planning to take a trip, particularly since there are so many restrictions involved. I discovered this when I called an airline the other day and said I wanted two seats to California.

'Very well. We can give you a special rate if you fly between Monday and Friday and promise not to smoke over Salt Lake City.'

'I promise. What rate can I get?'

'You don't happen to be an American Indian do you?'

'No.'

'That's too bad, because if you were an American Indian and left at four o'clock in the morning and returned at three o'clock the next morning, we could give you $33^1/_3$ per cent off.'

'Gee, that's too bad,' I said. 'Do you have any other special fares?'

'Here's one,' she said. 'It's good from Monday evening till Wednesday noon. If you're an American ambassador to any Scandinavian country and you're on home leave, you're entitled to first-class meals in the tourist section of the plane.'

'I'm afraid I wouldn't qualify for that. Incidentally, I'm travelling with my wife.'

'Well, why didn't you say so?' she said excitedly. 'Is she under twenty-one years of age?'

'I'm not sure,' I replied.

'Well, if she was and you both left on a weekday and neither of you had sinus conditions, you would be entitled to a discount.

'Of course, if she was pregnant and you both came from a state that didn't have an "O" in it, you could get an extra 5 per cent, unless this happened to be your first child.'

'I guess that eliminates us.'

'You give up too easily,' she said. 'Are either one of you students? If you were and happened to be studying animal husbandry at a land-grant college, I could give you each 45 per cent off, if you flew on Friday 13th.'

'I can't qualify for that one.'

'We still have some other special discount flights,' she said. 'If you're a Rhodes scholar majoring in the humanities and you have two children, you can take our coach service any time after midnight on the Fourth of July for one third less.'

'Couldn't you just make out two tickets to California at the regular rate?'

'I'm sorry,' she said, 'I've never made out that kind of ticket. You'll have to talk to my supervisor.'

Reprinted from *Son of the Great Society* (Weidenfeld and Nicolson) with the author's permission.

Best promotional 'own goal' by an airline

British Airways flew their own beauty queen, Kim Turner, aged twenty-three, to Cyprus in February 1980 for a public relations visit to launch their campaign 'We take good care of you'. On arrival they discovered they had rather dropped a brick. Miss Turner arrived in Cyprus looking stunning but simply did not have a thing to wear. Her luggage, including BA uniforms and cocktail dresses, had failed to travel with her from the Gloucester Road air terminal. The airline had taken good care of Miss Turner but not her suitcases. They were later found in that well-known gnome from home, Zurich.

Kingsley Amis

World-renowned author

Most memorable flight
I last took to the air in the summer of 1932 from Croydon Aerodrome and landed there again some ten minutes later. The fare was 5 shillings (25p) and the aircraft a De Havilland Dragon-Rapide. The whole enterprise seemed to me hazardous in the extreme.

I understand that the Dragon-Rapide has since been withdrawn from service, and that other developments have taken place, but I remain mistrustful.

Worst treatment of passengers by an airline

You will not be surprised to learn that I have had hundreds of nominations for this category, but perhaps few could beat the cautionary tale told by the Soviet weekly, the *Literary Gazette*, in November 1978 and recalled Julian Pettifer's TV tie-in *Diamonds in the Sky* (Bodley Head/BBC, 1979). The newspaper recorded how the scheduled Aeroflot flight from Moscow to the Far East was only half full so, in an effort to save roubles, it was cancelled. The passengers were told to remain in the terminal building, which was packed. Sitting on the floor and huddling in corners, they waited all night, and all the next day, completely starved of announcements. When the next Far East flight was finally called, some of the passengers were asleep and missed boarding. Aeroflot were the model of efficiency. They fined all those who had failed to turn up for the second flight 25 per cent of the fare before they could travel again.

Noisiest airport

My nomination for this is Brize Norton, departure point for some of my most venturesome flights including a 23½-hour marathon to Nellis AFB, Las Vegas, via RAF Honington, Wildenrath, Gander (what's sauce for Goose Bay) and Washington. The unique flavour of travelling from BZZ as thousands of service personnel will testify, is that flights inevitably leave between 3.00 and 4.30 a.m. This means a third of a night's attempted sleep at the world's most luxurious transit camp, euphemistically called 'Gateway House'.

As one leading general observed to me, the central heating at this establishment is always turned up so high that you are forced to open the windows. Having opened the windows it is then impossible to sleep for the unparalleled mega-decibel din of seventeen VC–10s simultaneously revving up outside as if part of a world Hell's Angel convention. This is all a ploy, of course, to make sure you sleep during one of the interminable (dry!) VC-10 flights and don't upset those nice RAF loadmasters.

Worst airport bureaucracy

Mr Simon Calder of south-east London told the magazine *Executive Travel* in September 1985 how he had been forced to spend an extra day in Bucharest, Rumania, after officials had decided to search his luggage. There was, you see, a snag. His luggage had already been loaded aboard the plane. With pristine Soviet bloc logic, the Rumanians thoughtfully decided that Mr Calder should stay with them until the plane had gone to London via Brussels, then returned, via Brussels once again, so they could look through his luggage once it had been offloaded.

Biggest-ever parking fine for a jet

A customized Boeing 707 was 'clamped' at Luton Airport in February 1984 after running up a massive £35,000 parking fine. The jet had been ordered by Saudi businessman Sheik bin Mirjis al Muraibidh, and was to have featured £750,000 worth of luxury couches, bedrooms, solid gold bath taps and seat buckles, together with the very latest video system free from the plane's interference. But the Sheik never went through with the order, and all the while the jet sat on the Luton tarmac clocking up parking fees of £6.50 an hour. The plane was later bought by a Manchester businessman for conversion into a restaurant for 'high-flyers' in Ashton New Road, Manchester. He said he'd be watching for traffic wardens.

Worst case of lost bearings

The Russians were just as surprised as anyone else when the plane carrying two top US generals touched down at their top-secret airfield in Armenia, in November 1970. It was the sort of incident that might have sparked off World War III, but the generals were released after convincing the Soviets that their plane was really meant for Kars in Eastern Turkey. The plane had landed in Russia after the pilot, generally a bit off course, mixed up two railway tracks which he had been following to pinpoint his position.

What made things embarrassing for the US top brass was that they stepped boldly out of their plane for a welcoming party safe in the knowledge that they had landed at a NATO airfield. The unhappy truth was only revealed when a vehicle appeared which did not have the Turkish star and crescent on it – only the large red star of the Soviet Union – and the accompanying officials turned out to be Russian soldiers carrying Kalashnikovs.

Worst visual landing

It was a gas! An American Boeing 707 in the 1960s managed to mistake tiny Northolt Airport, Middlesex, for its big brother Heathrow after a classic case of mistaken identity. One of the land-marks coming into Heathrow is the Southall gasometer. The pilot saw the gasometer, lowered his flaps and came in gracefully to land. There was just one little problem. It was the wrong gasometer. And the wrong airport. Instead of Heathrow he had landed at Northolt, fourteen miles away. What comes down does not necessarily go up just as easily, and virtually the whole plane had to be stripped to enable it to leave the ground again. Henceforth gasometers in the London area were emblazoned with the letters LHR and an arrow to show the correct way to errant high-speed pilots.

The only runway closed by heavy breathing

Instead of receiving landing instructions, pilots radioing a control tower at Roinsy Airport near Paris received a message which consisted wholly of the sounds of the grunts and groans of couples making love. No, a horde of Mile High Clubbers had *not* stormed the control tower. A pirate radio station had started up nearby, broadcasting heavy breathing and pornographic stories. This might not have been so bad if it had not blocked out trans-missions from the control tower. At first pilots came in to land 'blind' due to the radio sex sessions (I think I might have phrased that better). But as planes circled out of contact in the skies above, officials ruled that the runway be closed while a frantic police search was mounted to find the culprits. They were discovered, their equipment impounded (what equipment was unspecified) and the runway reopened to the more normal Oscar-Delta-Charlie and Rogering.

High Jinks

There's always plenty to do on a plane journey. Ask Rod Stewart, who held what he described as 'a hell of a party' aboard a British Airways flight from Los Angeles to London in December 1977. Other passengers said Mr Stewart's behaviour on the 10½-hour flight was 'appalling' and said he had caused 'havoc' and 'a riot'.

After the party the plane's first-class cabin was described as 'like a pigsty' and 'like Steptoe's backyard' with food, empty bottles and cigarette ends everywhere, the honey, jam and butter smeared over the seats, some of which were ripped.

On arrival the rock star and his entire thirteen-strong entourage were detained in the airport VIP lounge while statements were taken, and his musical arranger Mr Dave Horowitz, was charged with being drunk and disorderly, which later cost him a £25 fine.

'Sailing' down the airport steps with a girl and a large bottle of brandy in tow and singing 'I'd walk a million miles for one of your legs', Mr Stewart said, 'I don't think we behaved badly . . . On second thoughts, yes we did.'

But aeroplanes have always been the scene of 'high jinks'.

Most daring 'streak' at 30,000 feet

She was blonde and beautiful, and it wasn't too hard to spot that she had an all-over tan. The lady flung back the curtains separating first class on Flight 51 from Miami and Los Angeles in June 1978, and waving a bottle of champagne, laughing and giggling, set about exposing her ample charms to incredulous passengers.

It was clear that her happiness had spread to others in the cabin as she whooped a full-frontal toast and dashed towards the middle section of the DC-10. She then climbed on the front recliner and moved along the row, swinging a shapely leg over each of the six seats.

The lady was pursued by a flight steward with a blanket who tried an instant cover-up job, but she proved far too nimble for him.

After quaffing more champagne, our heroine perched on top of row 27 and announced: 'I've inherited five million dollars and I'm celebrating!' Her male travelling companion meanwhile hid under his stowed 'life-jacket in embarrassment.

National Airlines, the carrier, were a little upset by all this, especially as their advertising had promised passengers 'no frills travel'. It was definitely better than any in-flight movie, but said a spokesman sternly: 'It is not part of our standard entertainment.'

The most amazing debut as an in-flight entertainer by a leader of Her Majesty's Opposition

Labour leader Michael Foot 'flew into a storm' with a 'flight of fancy' in the words of the popular press when he staged two stand-up comedy spots on a delayed British Airways flight from Oslo to London. As the plane languished on the runway banter grew between Mr Foot and his fellow passengers, and he twice took hold of the plane's public-address system. The first was to attempt to end a hitch in the drinks supply to the increasingly distraught passengers, but the second degenerated into a political broadcast in which Mr Foot denounced Mrs Thatcher, said planes would never be late under a Socialist government, and that he and his co-pilot one Mr Ray Buckton would ensure that their journey was a safe one. A group of Norwegians on the plane were said to be 'nonplussed' at the display, which one passenger, Mr Desmond Nears-Crouch, labelled 'garbled and embarrassing'. Mr Foot (in mouth?) said it was all 'just a joke', but Mr Vivian Bendall, Conservative MP for Ilford North, tabled a Commons question asking for an explanation of what he headily called 'this breathtaking incident'.

Most memorable aerial photographs

These were taken by an American flight engineer called Mr Miller, who presented evidence to a Congressional sub-committee in 1956 suggesting that pilots were engaging in actions which could lead to mid-air collisions. Using a concealed camera in the cockpit, Mr Miller took 300 photographs in four years. Most pictured pilots and co-pilots peacefully asleep, but the most interesting showed 1) a stewardess sitting on the captain's lap when he was flying and 2) (no connection with 1)) the picture of a donkey wandering about the cabin in mid-flight. This, reported Mr Miller, had been brought aboard by a group of drunken convention delegates who then proceeded to strip the plane of its furnishings.

Yes, don't worry, things have been tightened up in the flight deck and, since 1970, all airlines have carried freshly oat-filled nosebags and shovels in case of unexpected equine passengers.

Les Dawson

Leading comedian and host of 'Blankety Blank'

Favourite airline
British Airways, incredible as it may appear, mainly due to a rather sensuous stewardess who gave me a faint twitch of hope in the carnal sense and helped me off the plane after a bout with a sort of sinister gin.

Least favourite airline
Memory shudders at this. I think the airline was called LIAT in the West Indies. The plane was somewhat elderly – it was an early jet – a bag of charcoal and an oven – and it had a secret passage.

Funniest moment
A woman in a large crepe hat with matching surgical stockings who said cheerfully: 'One thing about these VC-10 s, they only crash once.'

Most amazing experience
Never been sober enough to observe.

Most unusual aerial wedding

It was a case of really going down the aisle when Edward 'Doc' Williams, portly fifty-two-year-old millionaire boss of a chain of American cemeteries and Marian Sutton, a twenty-five-year-old cover girl, staged a grave but exotic wedding in the orchid-bedecked tail section of a chartered jet 5000 feet above the cornfields of Iowa.

But it wasn't just for effect. The aerial nuptials bypassed a strict Minnesota divorce law which insisted on a six-month waiting period after the granting of a decree. 'Doc' Williams had been separated from his wife for just four weeks.

Behind the airliner, chartered at a cost of $5000, a sky-writing plane scrawled 'just married' and traced arrows pierced with hearts in the sky with a series of vapour trails. Thankfully they thought twice about attaching tin cans to the back of the plane.

The three most excruciating jokes from the film *Airplane*

Can you fly this plane and land it?
– Surely you can't be serious.
I am serious . . . And don't call me Shirley.

> Leslie Nielsen (Dr Rumack) to
> Robert Hays (Ted Striker)

Striker: Mayday! Mayday! Mayday!
McCroskey: Mayday? What the hell is that for?
Johnny: Mayday – that's the Russian New Year. We'll have a big parade and serve hot hors d'oeuvre . . .

> Robert Hays, Lloyd Bridges
> and Stephen Stucker

Excuse me, sir, there's a little problem up in the cockpit.
– The cockpit! What is it?
Oh, it's a little room up in the front of the plane where the pilot sits.

> Lorna Patterson (Randy) to Robert Hays (Ted Striker)

Best XXXXing record aloft

When Australian Test wicketkeeper Rodney Marsh arrived in London for the start of the 1983 World Cup series, he hardly cut a dashing figure in his smart tour togs and cap as he was helped off the plane by two team-mates looking monumentally worse for the journey. There was the inevitable fracas with photographers. Much later it was revealed by colleague Dennis Lillee (*Lillee, Over and Out*, Methuen, 1984) that behind Mr Marsh's anguish lay a spectacular feat of record-breaking. The doughty keeper had, believe it or not, managed to win the blue riband of Anglo-Antipodean travel, beating the world record for the number of cans of lager consumed between Kingsford Smith Airport, Sydney, and Heathrow Airport, London. The record had previously stood at forty-four cans.

'The training he put into the preparation for his attempt on the drinking record was something to behold,' said an admiring Lillee in his book. 'He tackled it with such relish and gusto that I was afraid he might kill himself before the air hostess was able to say, "Fasten your seat belts, please." '

Mr Lillee went on to describe lovingly how each can was sunk. 'Can No.43 arrived and was duly despatched ... not with the same finesse, as, say, number 14. The wrist was somewhat less fluent; in fact as the plane's nose tilted in its Heathrow approach, I swear to this day I could see beer about to spill over his bottom teeth onto the floor.

'No. 44 was your standard-sized can, but to Rodney it must have looked as big as a bucket . . . he somehow focused on it, guided it to his mouth and sipped . . . "I can't make it," Rodney pleaded in a voice which sounded as if he had a mouthful of marbles . . . "Bullshit!" we chorused.'

Mr Lillee observed that the challenge had by now 'assumed all the significance of the Ashes'.

'We tilted Rodney's head back and literally forced him. He gurgled, he gasped, he grunted and he growled. But by God, he drank it.'

An announcement was then made: 'Ladies and gentlemen, I now give you the new heavyweight beer-drinking champion of the cricket world.' There was the inevitable cheering but poor Mr Marsh could hear none of it.

Said Lillee: 'There was no need for him to have landed with his seat belt buckled. The plane could have run into a mountain without dislodging him from his seat. He was history. Drunk as a monkey. Iron Gloves – they should have called him Iron Guts!'

Most atmospheric first-division soccer match

In June 1984 police were despatched to meet South African Airways Flight 234 carrying soccer stars from Liverpool and Tottenham Hotspur from a sponsored match in Swaziland. The captain had complained that players from the two clubs had staged their own version of the Cup Final at a height of 35,000 feet with a 'kickabout' in the aisle. Liverpool's Footballer of the Year, Ian Rush, said: 'We had a few drinks and were having a good laugh. Then suddenly a steward came up and told us to keep the noise down. He said other passengers were trying to get some sleep.' It's never the same without David Coleman.

Most champagne consumed in aviation history

This record was established on Virgin Atlantic Airlines' inaugural run to New York in June 1984, together with several more 'firsts' in the rear seats of the 'love is in the air' variety. In addition to gallons of gin, whisky, vodka and brandy, an astonishing 720 bottles of champagne were accounted for by the invited horde of showbiz and press revellers. One newspaper described the journey as 'Branson's pickle', but my own spy, Christopher Biggins, tells me why so much champagne: 'The press were stuffing bottles in their suitcases. Greedy buggers!'

Worst-ever smoking row

It was described as 'like a scene from *Airplane*' when a TWA jumbo flying from Athens to New York with more than 300 people on board made an emergency landing at Heathrow Airport after a full-scale punch-up in the passenger cabin.

Fists started flying, as well as the passengers and crew, when fifty-two-year-old Steven Varvaris, of Jackson, Mississippi, refused to put out a cigar after a request from the cabin staff. (Cigarettes are allowed in airliners, but not cigars or pipes.) Mr

Varvaris then became embroiled in a full-blown brawl.

The captain decided to make an emergency landing at London, but this only brought more drama. The first time he came in to land, the 747 overshot the runway. The second time, it made the landing, but as police dashed aboard to seize Mr Varvaris, a seventy-seven-year-old woman collapsed and had to be taken to hospital with liver failure.

The flight eventually took off several hours later. The cigar row smouldered on for another three

---

Christopher Biggins

Actor/presenter

Best airline
British Airways. Because all the staff who work on the airline are British and of course recognize you, so you get that extra-special treatment.

Worst airline
The airline that goes to the Isle of Man because they only have two flights a day, one early in the morning and one in the evening.

Craziest flight
During the inaugural Virgin Atlantic flight to New York. The party was so good that halfway over the Atlantic I thought I'd had enough and should really go home. Thank God someone stopped me leaving by the door.

---

weeks, until the defence at Uxbridge magistrates' court asked for an assault charge against Mr Varvaris to be withdrawn.

The court heard how the financial consequences for lighting up his Havana had been 'devastating'. His wife, who had continued on the original flight, had spent £700 returning to give evidence for her husband and they had spent £760 on hotel expenses living in London waiting for the full case to be heard. Mr Varvaris had, on being arrested, spent a week in jail. He was awarded unspecified costs.

'It was a mighty expensive cigar,' said a police spokesman. Mr Varvaris seemed pleased with the result, lighting up a large Corona on being freed. Minutes later he was involved in another incident, however, huffing at press photographers, and throwing a dustbin at them.

Most unusual hijack (1)

The captain of a British cargo plane flying over Orly Airport, Paris, requested permission to land after his airliner was 'hijacked' by 300 monkeys. He radioed the control tower: 'I have no mechanical difficulty but my passengers are creating a serious disturbance.'

When the plane landed, two stewardesses who did not know the source of the trouble rushed to the jet. They saw that the cabin was unlit, and hearing screams, thought there had been injuries among the passengers. On boarding they were immediately pounced on by the monkeys, who had escaped from their crates en route for London Zoo from Brindisi. The girls leaped from the plane, now screaming themselves. It was hours before the monkeys were rounded up.

Barbara Cartland

*Leading novelist, socialite and health-food
enthusiast*

Most memorable flight
Flying was the main interest of the young and
dashing in 1931. Early that summer a clever
young man, later a successful author, called Ian
Davison, two young Air Force pilots, Flying
Officer E.L. Mole and Flying Officer E.O. Wanliss
and myself became thrilled with the idea of
towing a glider by aeroplane then releasing it when
it was high enough to glide any distance required.
This seemed to me to be an excellent and cheap
proposition for commercial flying. There had been
gliding contests since 1923 but in 1930 new
improvements had been perfected. Why not a
train of gliders for light commodities to be dropped
off like slip coaches at various ports of call? To
show the possibility of this we arranged to build a
glider, tow it to 10,000 feet and let it fly the
Channel, landing on a French aerodrome.
   I gave the order for the glider to be started and
we kept very quiet as to what we were planning.
But someone talked and a month later the *Daily
Mail* announced an offer of a £1000 prize to the
first glider to fly the Channel both ways. It was
soon obvious that there would be a rush across

the Channel on the day chosen and the whole thing would be turned into a 'stunt'.

Accordingly, I decided not to compete but to do something quite different. The maker of my glider, however, was competing himself and taking no chances. By a strange coincidence it was quite impossible for the glider to be ready even twenty-four hours before the day of the race.

So, from Manston Aerodrome on 20 June we let the Channel competitor start first, then when the released cable was dropped back to us, we attached it to the aeroplane in which I sat and to the red-and-white 'Barbara Cartland', and turning our backs on the coast set off across country to deliver the first aeroplane-towed glider mail.

We sailed smoothly across the green face of England, a cricket match was stopped to wave to us as we passed, golfers stared at us from the fairways of famous courses, the world was very beautiful and we were excited at what we were achieving.

With no mishaps we reached Reading Aerodrome, a distance of about 100 miles, where the mayor was waiting to greet us.

We flew back in style – with a five aeroplane escort.

In 1984 I received America's Bishop Wright Air Industry Award at Kennedy Airport for my contribution to the development of aviation when, in 1931 I and two RAF officers thought of, and carried, the first aeroplane-towed glider air mail.

Most unusual hijack (2)

Six mink escaped from a crate and held seventy passengers and crew at bay for eighteen hours at New York International Airport. Reuter reported they had 'taken possession of the plane', and it took almost a whole day to recapture them. Their hijack demands were not published.

Most unusual hijack (3)

Three lions took control of a Dart Herald airliner of Swiss Globe Airlines in July 1966, forcing an emergency landing at Brussels Airport and launching a full-scale emergency alert. The three lions were being taken from Addis Ababa, Ethiopia, to the Marquess of Bath's estate at Longleat, Wilts, when they gnawed through the wooden bars of their cages and invaded the flight deck. The pilot, Captain Paul Wurhman, aged thirty-six, was talking to Brussels control when he felt 'something warm and wet' around his heels.

'I called "Brussels, Brussels, emergency landing please. Three lions in my cockpit". The control replied: "Stick 'em in your petrol tank," ' he said later.

But controllers finally believed Captain Wurhman when they heard scuffling (the sound of the co-pilot trying to keep the big cats at bay with an axe) and then the sound of a lion's roar into the radio set.

When the plane landed police were standing by with sub-machine and foam guns. Huge nets were thrown over the plane, but later the lions were captured in smaller nets by a brave lady keeper from Antwerp Zoo. These big cats always have an eye for the mane chance.

Worst-ever no smoking row

The captain described what took place as 'an insurrection' after passengers became embroiled in one of the most heated rows in aviation history in December 1979 – all over a man who insisted on a no-smoking seat.

The abstemiously named Mr Richard Lent, a non-smoking Washington lawyer, inflamed passions after he climbed aboard the 8 a.m. Eastern Airlines shuttle to Washington and sat down in the middle of the aircraft, several rows forward of the section reserved for non-smokers. He asked the stewardess if the non-smoking area could be extended forward to embrace his seat.

Mr Lent clearly knew the law. American airlines can be fined heavily for not complying with a passenger's request to be seated in a no-smoking seat. The stewardess tried to find a compromise by asking if anyone would swap places with him. They wouldn't. She asked Mr Lent if he would mind travelling on the next shuttle ten minutes later. He said he would mind. He, after all, being a lawyer, knew his rights. The stewardess had no choice but to accede to his request and extend the non-smoking area forward to his seat.

Not surprisingly, a lot of passengers who had been waiting to light up their first cigarette of the day were incensed by this. 'They perceived that they were being prevented from doing so by just one man,' said Mr Gil Perlroth, Eastern Airlines spokesman. Tempers became heated. 'We're not giving up for Lent,' they shouted.

When the plane took off, some passengers defiantly started smoking, blowing the smoke over their enemy. There followed a furious slanging match.

By now tempers were well alight. The captain, hearing the row going on behind him, warned the protagonists to stop. 'This insurrection has got to stop or I'm going to land this aircraft,' he fumed. It didn't stop. He landed the aircraft at Baltimore, just thirty-nine miles from where the passengers had begun their flight, and defiantly put them all out.

Dave Wetzel

GLC Transport Committee Chairman and former Heathrow union convener

Favourite air story

This used to be the favourite tale of all at British Airways. Just after the war, BEA used to fly De Havilland Rapides to Jersey. The plane was an eight-seater with passengers placed either side of the gangway, and just one pilot's seat at the front. One BEA pilot was a real practical joker and his favourite trick was to walk up to the aeroplane in an old mac, wearing dark sunglasses and carrying a white stick, as if he were blind. He would plonk down in a seat at the rear and after a long pause announce, 'Well if no one else is going to fly this ruddy thing, I will', before stumbling up to the cockpit bumping into all the by-now horrified passengers on the way.

Most outrageous pop-star passenger

My award for this goes to Keith Moon, late, lamented drummer of The Who, who carried his penchant for smashing up hotel rooms to the skyways. A typical example came in July 1978, on a plane about to leave Mauritius for the Seychelles. After running up and down the plane uttering oaths, 'Moon the Loon' burst into the flight deck and began an impromptu drum session on the engineer's control panel. Airport officials were called and he was dragged screaming from the plane after being

declared 'unfit to travel' by a doctor. On the way, Moon tried to ground the aircraft by throwing his briefcase at the engine (he missed) and shouting: 'If I can't go, nobody can. Fetch the press!' A spokesman for the group apologized to passengers and said Mr Moon was suffering from the after-effects of taking sleeping pills, which his girlfriend had given him. An airline official said: 'Just *who* the hell does he think he is?'

The champion transatlantic air hostess bottom-slapper of all time

This honour goes to the inappropriately named Mr Aubrey Bumguard, aged forty-five, of Galveston, Texas. In February 1977 Mr Bumguard found himself charged with air piracy for slapping the rear parts of two National Airlines hostesses on a flight between London and Miami.

Mr Bumguard had taken the airline's slogan – 'TAKE ME, I'M YOURS' – a little too far, a preliminary court hearing in Miami heard.

Stewardess Miss Patti Dewoody said she received four slaps in all, and one was so strong she almost fell. 'I told him each time "cut that out" but he just mimicked me,' she said. She added she did not consider the slaps 'a flirtatious advance'.

Miss Jane Otto said Bumguard slapped her backside twice, and after the third slap she complained to the pilot who warned him to stop. 'But shortly afterwards I felt another slap on my behind and I had to turn and confront him again.'

Miss Otto said he seemed to have had too many drinks. 'I thought he might be a problem,' she said.

The Customer Is Always Tight

Passengers can be a problem. There was, for instance, the incredible case of the elderly couple who disappeared in the middle of their flight. A frantic search by the cabin staff of the whole fuselage and the lavatories failed to find the errant twosome. Finally two bundles of what appeared to be blankets on the luggage rack were turned over . . . and there they were. They had thought the rack – tiny though it was – was a row of bunk beds for them to turn into when it got dark outside.

Among other favourite passenger stories collected by one airline:

* The woman passenger from China who brought some live lobsters aboard. Halfway through the flight they escaped to claw their way over the seats one by one, terrifying sleeping airtravellers.

* The old lady who tried to force her way into the hold of a jumbo jet because 'I want to take my dog for a walk'.

* The dowager duchess who, at the stroke of 8 p.m., tried 'to go upstairs to the dining hall'.

The worst prose ever penned in praise of flying

My accolade goes to Ian Hunter of the group Mott the Hoople who in 1974 had the nerve to unleash on his unsuspecting fans a mind-boggling work called *Diary of a Rock 'n' Roll Star* (Panther). It contains the following tribute to the world of commercial aviation:

'For those of you who have never flown, I can tell you it's a buzz if you can dig it. You get free meals, drinks and papers, duty-free gifts and fags (200 Benson & Hedges for £1.50) and they get good wages to treat you like royalty ... My little window is up now and a moon-like surface greets my eyes ... Looking down at that land of clouds – you want to jump out and play in them and jump up and down. The seats recline and they even have movies. For a pound you can get earphones which when plugged in give a variety of music for every taste plus the sound track of the movie – which ain't bad.'

It ain't bad compared with your hexcruciating prose, mate. I think if I had the misfortune to travel with Mr Hunter I'd be tempted to jump out into the clouds there and then.

Most lunatic behaviour at the check-in

Former 'Who' roadie Dougal (Peter) Butler tells in his devastating tome *Moon the Loon* (Star, 1981) how the most outrageous rock drummer in the world became a little bored when the plane he was due to catch from Glasgow was diverted to Prestwick. Mr Moon began, it appears, to take this out on passengers during the coach journey to Ayrshire, stomping up and down the aisle shouting 'Fares, please', 'Move on down the car, please' and 'City centre next stop'. Not quite satisfied with this he then divested the old lady sitting in the front seat of her wig, and persuaded the driver to take his hand off the steering wheel and swig from a bottle of Courvoisier on pain of being hijacked to Cuba.

A further delay at the check-in led the bored fur-clad Loon to commandeer a wheelchair in which he propelled himself at great speed round the airport, with a cassette tape of the Beach Boys blaring at full volume to drown out all the flight announcements. ('He looked most professional and might well have been a kosher invalid,' said the admiring Mr Butler.) The drummer was chased by two security guards, but managed to escape them by successfully piloting his wheelchair down a long flight of stairs, landing upright, and scuttling off.

Then disaster! The Beach Boys tape ran out, reported Mr Butler sombrely, and Mr Moon became *extremely* bored, first throwing his cassette player at a tobacconist's window (to his amazement it bounced straight back at him) and then trying to hold up the old lady who ran it with a toy gun emitting a flag emblazoned BANG!

Felony was averted, reported Mr Butler, when the old lady fainted ('You miserable old boot,' shouted Moon), but the security forces were further kept at bay by the famous drummer, now wielding his pistol like a professional and shouting 'Bang! Bang!'

Unsurprisingly, Mr Moon was arrested and, according to Mr Butler, 'carted off to the cooler' where he was 'sprung' by 'a large quantity of cash'. He was returned to the check-in counter to resume his flight, but 'when the airport security force attempt to put the collective arm upon him in order that he may offend no more users of the British Airports Authority facilities', extreme boredom returned once more.

Says Mr Butler: 'Moon became so violent that he pushes over one of the check-in desk computer terminals. It falls to the floor with spluttering noises and just before the screen goes dead, it books thirty-two Mormons on a massage parlour tour of Bangkok.'

Biggest in-flight loser

This was believed to be the American company chairman, too embarrassed to give his name, who in November 1978 lost his shirt and $10,000 on a flight from New York to Heathrow. The man who took most of the money, Texan oil worker Tom Purdy, said: 'We started playing poker about a half-hour after take-off and the last hand was played as we touched down in New York.' The loser – down £14 a minute during the six-hour flight – vowed, 'My old lady would give me hell if she knew about this. From now on I am flying Concorde. Then if I get in a game there will be only three and a half hours to lose my money.'

The longest cross-Channel crossing

American tourist John Coker couldn't understand why there was so much water in the English Channel. And when he grasped the button for the stewardess, his worst fears were confirmed. He wasn't, after all, making the short hop from London to Frankfurt, after a stopover at Heathrow en route from Detroit. Instead he was heading back the way he had come – back across the Atlantic, this time to Washington, DC.

Mr Coker's marathon in April 1979 ended after thirty-six hours when he had criss-crossed the Atlantic three times and had had eight meals aboard four different airliners. A slip-up by a Pan

Am check-in girl had sent him not across the Channel but on a 7730–mile round voyage.

He said: 'It's a different way of spending Easter.'

Lord Bottomley

Formerly Labour's Minister of Overseas Development

Favourite airline

Any which gets me safely to my destination on time! I am glad to say that most airlines on which I have travelled fall into this category. The best air travel I have ever experienced, however, was on a Short's Sunderland Flying Boat from Britain to India in 1946. It was like a floating hotel. And sadly, no more!

Most chastening experience

My wife and I were in a South African Air Force machine – a Ventura – which was flying us back to Cape Town from East London. After we had started our journey, visibility became very bad, and as we neared Cape Town we had to fly very low and between the mountains. Finally we got through the hills and then the pilot had to go out to sea and searched along the coast for his destination. The best was yet to come though – the co-pilot had to stand on the seat and put his head out through the look-out in an endeavour to locate our position!

Briefest-ever round trip to the United States

Dr John Follows, aged eighty, splashed out £600 for a return trip to America from Corfe Mullen, Dorset, in March 1984, to see his daughter in South Carolina. But when he arrived at New York's Kennedy Airport he realized he had forgotten her name and address. Dr Follows caught the next plane back, two hours later. That was not, however, the end of the affair. His non-appearance in South Carolina sparked off a police hunt after his daughter reported him missing. Back at home in Dorset the absent-minded doctor said: 'I was tired and confused when I arrived.'

Shortest visit to London by a Jamaican belly-dancer

Exotic dancer Cynthia Nelson had intended to make the short hop from Kingston, Jamaica, to Montego Bay in September 1974. Instead she found herself at Heathrow Airport, London, some 5000 miles away. Unfortunately all she had with her was £2 in Jamaican dollars and a spare pair of knickers in her handbag. Miss Nelson was in London for just one hour before being returned to the West Indies. She said: 'I thought the plane seemed to be in the air for a long time.'

The only man to ground an airliner with his stomach

We've all dreaded being plonked in the seat next to the twenty-two-stone giant who's the largest man on the flight. Spare a thought for the eighty-three passengers on a Dublin to London jet in June 1967, who went nowhere for an hour because of one man's giant girth.

The jumbo-sized airfarer identified only as 'Mr Big' grounded the Aer Lingus plane when it was found he couldn't be strapped into his seatbelt. Just as the plane was about to take off, stewardess Anne O'Connell noticed he was not belted up. A search for the extra-large extending seatbelt each plane

carries proved fruitless, and the plane had to taxi back to the hangars for a new wide-bodied seat to be installed by mechanics.

Aer Lingus said: 'It wasn't our fault. Rules are very strict about all passengers having seatbelts fastened before take-off.'

Passenger most desperate for a cigarette

This honour goes to businessman John Johnson who, on a bus-stop flight from Atlantic City to New York in January 1986, was told by the steward to put out his rolled mellow Virginia. After a row he reluctantly agreed. But what happened next aboard the Allegheny Airlines jet had the sixty passengers fearing for their lives. Johnson suddenly leapt from his seat shouting 'I just have to have a smoke', and rushed to the flight deck. There he tore the radio headphones from the pilot's head and demanded that he overrule the steward and allow him to light up.

Captain Philip Griggs, not surprisingly, told him this was against regulations (No. 33: passengers shall not rip headphones from the ears of the pilot whilst the plane is in motion) and ordered him back to his seat. The next thing he knew Johnson had grabbed the controls.

Said Captain Griggs: 'We were at 40,000 feet and the plane fell more than 2000 feet before my co-pilot managed to get it out of a spin.'

Help was at hand though. Two other passengers piled into Johnson and, thankfully, were able to extinguish his frenzy by knocking him out. On landing (safely!) he was arrested.

Gorden Kaye

Actor and star of "Allo, 'allo'

Most amusing flight
This happened within my earshot. On a five-hour
flight from Boston to Los Angeles a man on the
seat across the aisle had had one or two drinks too
many. When the stewardess brought his meal, she
planted it in front of him. He looked at her rather
reserved expression, tugged her sleeve and said,
'Smile! can't you?' 'I will if you will,' said the girl.
The man beamed inanely. 'Now hold that for five
hours,' she said and sailed off with her trolley.

Funniest story
This was told to me. John Gregson, the actor, was
terrified of flying and went everywhere by boat,
train or car. He had been filming in Europe and
had just arrived back in London after a long train
journey and Channel crossing, when he received a
phone call. Urgent post dubbing was required and
could he get back to Vienna that day. The only
way was by air so he 'loaded' himself up with
alcohol as the flight progressed. A passing steward
recognized him and engaged him in the usual
small talk eventually surmising that the actor
must fly a lot. 'Oh yes,' lied Gregson, 'I love it.'
'Mmm,' said the steward, 'most people do. If only
they knew by how delicate a thread their life was
held, they'd have a coronary.' Rumour had it that
Gregson had to be taken from the aircraft by
stretcher.

Most spectacular demonstration by stranded passengers

This came in August 1977 when three women, protesting at delays at London's Heathrow Airport due to catering and air traffic controllers' strikes, marched down a taxiway and tried to block the path of a jumbo jet which had just landed. The captain was described as having had 'the fright of his life' (yes, they were big girls), but managed to brake hard and veer off course so his plane was, thankfully, undamaged.

One of the women, who were among 100 stranded on a Nigerian Airways charter flight, said: 'This was the only way of getting the airline to listen to us. We were aware of the dangers but we were desperate.' While the women staged their protest, another sixty passengers stormed the charter Boeing 707 and staged a 'sit-in'. It left soon afterwards – more than twenty-four hours late.

Most eccentric travelling couple

Mr D. Bass was travelling with his friend from London to Auckland in June 1973, when he suddenly went missing. Mr Bass's fellow passengers sat in the sweltering heat of Kuala Lumpur Airport for nearly an hour while the airline called his name over the loudspeakers. The captain said he would not leave unless he had a full complement of passengers. The other passengers grew more and more irate.

The captain hit upon the bright idea of a luggage identification parade, and it was only then that the friend of Mr D. Bass stepped forward. He was a musician and he realized that the 'piece of luggage' he had bought a £355.55 economy-class ticket for had disappeared.

'Where's my *double bass*?' he boomed to the stewardess. 'It's supposed to be on this seat next to me.'

Fortunately, it turned out that Mr D. Bass had not strummed off by himself to take in the delights of Kuala Lumpur. Realizing he was a passenger of some value, the outgoing stewardess had locked him in the lavatory to stop any harm befalling him at the hands of the Malaysian airport's cleaners. The absent-minded musician had wandered off and forgotten all about his valuable travelling companion. A friend said: 'He's always been highly strung.'

Most unusual passenger

In February 1984 travel agent Ruben Flores sent a stuffed bull on a 1000–mile flight as a paying cabin passenger. He reckoned it saved him almost £100. He found the cost of freighting the stuffed beast to his sister in Newark, New Jersey, as air cargo was £200. An airline seat cost £119. So he 'took the bull by the horns'.

Most unusual passenger on Concorde

When balding superstar crooner Art Garfunkel flew into London in March 1985, he forgot an essential part of his stage act – his toupee. When he stamped his foot and insisted he would not go on stage without it, his record company arranged to fly over the missing hairpiece – strapped to a £2000 seat on Concorde. The toupee was able to enjoy the best in-flight service, as well as the very latest Hollywood movie.

'Nothing is too much to keep our artists happy,' said a spokesman for Mr Garfunkel's record company.

Twelve house rules for the super-seasoned traveller (SST)

We've all seen them ... and don't they make us squirm. Every move planned to prove that they travel more than we do (and to more exotic places).

1. An SST never appears to rush, but with the aid of long John Cleese-style strides is *always* first to the plane. Any doubt about this is dispelled by special Concorde-style extending elbows which at the vital moment of embarkation, block the path of errant women and children foolishly mounting a challenge.

2. On entering the plane the SST extends his territory by draping as many items of hand baggage and clothing as practicable over neighbouring seats. These are only removed with extreme pique and a deep sigh loud enough to be heard throughout the plane.

3. Obligatory signs of membership of the SST fraternity are displayed. Concorde labels on the hand baggage are a must, as is one of the following newspapers: *Financial Times, Wall Street Journal, International Herald Tribune*.

4. An SST never takes a window seat, and would never dream of looking out of the plane to display a childish interest in other aircraft, aeroplanes, landing lights, etc. He takes up an aisle seat with one foot and the hand clutching his newspaper extended to jab into other passengers to prove how

inconvenient it is they should be travelling on his plane.

5.   On boarding, the SST fixes the stewards and stewardesses with an icy glare and does not waste time, breath or energy by repeating the trivial pleasantries such as 'Good morning'.

6.   On assuming his seat the SST will recline it with a surprise jerk and maximum force, thus warning the passenger behind there is more where that came from if he is in any way disturbed by smoke, laughter or idle chatter.

7.   The SST continues to read his newspaper through the safety demonstration. He is such an experienced traveller that this is, of course, quite meaningless. On no account will he read the safety leaflet in front of him. For extra effect, he may remove the air-sickness bag from the seat pocket, look at it disdainfully, screw it into a tiny ball, and throw the resulting mass down the aisle behind him.

8.   When the SST is offered a newspaper, he makes an impossible request like 'South China Morning Post' or 'Rio de Janeiro Gazette'. When apologies are offered he shrugs and complains loudly: 'Really, this airline has gone so far downhill since they introduced tourist class.'

9.   While everyone else waits thirstily for the drinks trolley the SST feigns total disinterest. He may take a whisky or gin while continuing to read his newspaper. Meals, too, are picked at with complete indifference, using one fork held languidly. The newspaper must be studied throughout.

10.   On take-off the SST again shows complete unconcern while all others are gripping their chair arms. A shrug of the shoulder or raised eyebrow is

permissible once the plane has climbed to cruising altitude.

11. Any heretic attempt by fellow passengers to open a conversation with the SST is put down with the response: 'I travel 300,000 miles a year. I suppose you just go once a year to Benidorm.' (Any subsequent reply is ignored.)

12. On disembarkation the SST again fixes the stewards and stewardesses with an icy stare and totally refuses to acknowledge the exhortation to 'have a nice day . . . thank you for travelling with us'. He may, however, mutter under his breath: 'It was your pleasure, hardly mine.'

Michael Grade

Controller, BBC1

Favourite airline
El Al – you don't buy a ticket, you give a donation.

Least favourite
Swissair – they give a new meaning to the word brusque.

Craziest flight
I once caught a flight that left on time and arrived early.

Most bizarre experience
Staying awake through an in-flight movie.

Most aggressive passenger

There were strange looks at the Australian property owner, Mrs June Morrison, aged fifty-three, as she walked up the aisle smelling of drink and singing 'Waltzing Matilda'. There were stranger looks when she began picking her teeth with an army knife. And there were still stranger looks when she leapt up and buried the knife into the head of the passenger sitting in front of her, Mr Nicholas Cantill, a fifty-three-year-old company director. Fined £750 with £300 costs by Staines magistrates' court in September 1980, the woman blamed 'claustrophobia' and was 'so shocked' by her own behaviour she said she had vowed never to fly again. (Thank heavens for that!)

Most plastered passengers

Three plastered holidaymakers grounded a charter jet at Munich Airport in 1970 after officials ruled ninety-seven able-bodied men and women plus three with plaster casts didn't go into 100 seats. The 100 holidaymakers had gone on a skiing holiday, but a trio had returned for the return leg with broken limbs. International flight rules are rules, said airport officials. Those in plaster casts require the legal minimum leg room, i.e., two seats.

The plane could not take off with legs stretching across the aisles or lying across their neighbours' laps. The three were invited to 'leg it'. A woman passenger said, 'It was like a scene from a Brian Rix farce (see p.66) – everybody swopping seats and scratching their heads. One girl wore a mini skirt and had great difficulty preserving her dignity while everybody heaved her leg about.'

Brian Rix

King of stage farce, now Secretary General of MENCAP

Most memorable flight

It was a freezing cold evening and as we climbed on board the Aquila seaplane on Southampton water in January 1952 it seemed even colder. Rugs were issued, for there was no heat in the cabin. For the uninitiated amongst you, Aquila Airways had acquired a few old Coastal Command Sunderlands. Not exactly speedy and not exactly comfortable on the old ears, for the cabins were not pressurized. Furthermore, the flight to Madeira took eight hours.

Suddenly we were moving, being towed out to our start mark. The engines spluttered into life, then a surge forward and we were off. At least that was the intention. As we thundered up the waterway it was quite clear that the Sunderland had no intention of taking off on that run. We stayed firmly splashing about in the water and slowly gurgled to a halt.

Twice more we beat up the water. Twice more we came to a shuddering, splashing halt.

Seven hours later, we did take off to start the long bumpy journey to our Paradise Isle.

You effete modern air travellers probably think these brown paper bags in front of you are for sandwiches. We older hands know better. Every passenger except one, me, was using their sick bag continually throughout that awful trip. I was determined to be the odd man out and sat with

clenched jaw below greenish cheeks for the entire journey. At last we landed in Funchal harbour; unfortunately there was a considerable swell and we were on the water for at least three quarters of an hour, waiting for the boat.

Clenched jaw and stiff-upper lip not withstanding I just had to use that brown paper bag. (I did feel sorry for the hostesses. They'd spent all day cleaning up the mess and now I had to complete the full house.)

Exactly a year later the wing of an Aquila Airways seaplane sank and the passengers had to scramble out on to the other wing to balance the plane and stop it going under. If that had happened to us we could have sat back and used our sick bags for ballast!

Retold from *My Farce from My Elbow* by Brian Rix (Sidgwick and Jackson,) with the author's permission.

The plane eventually took off after a three-hour delay, when three passengers volunteered to stay behind to give the plastered threesome their statutory leg room.

Most confused passenger

He was carrying a box of chocolates and looked ready for a delayed Christmas celebration when he strolled into the airport lounge at Heathrow, London. Yet he was not quite dressed for the part – a yellow shirt and flannels – spoke little English, and the ticket he was carrying was from Los Angeles to Manila, via Tokyo.

'Where do you think you are?' an airport official asked Mr Jose Cayatania.

'Tokyo,' said our friend. 'I'm changing planes to go home to Manila.'

Poor Mr Cayatania, whose luggage was 5000 miles away, would not be shaken and made to realize he was in London after choosing the wrong departure gate – the illusion being sustained by a planeload of Japanese arriving to board a flight to . . . Tokyo.

It took some time to persuade him to travel on a plane to Hong Kong, where he would be able to pick up a flight to Manila, and deliver his chocolates.

Hungriest passenger

A twenty-two-year-old American student, en route from Philadelphia to London in a TWA jumbo jet in February 1975, obviously didn't care much for the food. He began asking passengers if they liked Jesus and ended by biting four of them, three men and a woman. Stewardesses tried to placate him by offering him dinner instead, but finally he had to be handcuffed and restrained in his seat. On landing, police were put aboard to arrest him. An airport official said later: 'He appeared to be very hungry and ate a large meal after seeing the doctor.'

Least believable illegal immigrant

In his book *Airport International* (Macmillan, 1978) Brian Moynahan tells the story of Mr Asraf Mohammed Ali, a Pakistani from Karachi, who tried to enter Britain illegally claiming he was wanted for trial as a centre forward by a top London soccer club.

He made three mistakes. First was to give the name of his intending purchasers as Woolwich Queen's Park Athletic, having unfortunately mixed up the names of Arsenal, Charlton Athletic and QPR.

The second was the letter of invitation from 'WQPR'. It had no letterhead, and had even more spelling mistakes than could be expected.

The third was his age. Although claiming to be twenty-three, Ali was clearly in his forties and his poor physical condition suggested an unlikely block-buster signing to set the first division alight.

This Is Your Captain Sleeping

In one of the airlines' spicier tales, a TWA jet flight from Heathrow to New York had to be cancelled in October 1985 after the co-pilot and flight engineer became locked overnight in an Indian restaurant. The 300 passengers had to be rebooked on other airlines.

The two officers had been among the last customers of the Indian restaurant in Kensington, and had emerged from the lavatory to find the entire building in darkness. Unfortunately the staff had gone home and locked up, and the two men spent the night hammering on the doors and shouting for assistance. It was to no avail. At last, at 7 a.m., a police constable heard their cries and summoned the manager.

TWA said they had to cancel the flight because the crew had not had the required sleep to complete their statutory rest period. There was no replacement crew, so the passengers had to be put aboard other aircraft.

Yes, we're all depending on the men in the cockpit . . .

Loftiest barb against a pilot

Prince Philip's abilities as a flyer were the subject of an acid put-down by the Queen during small-talk

71

with a guest at Buckingham Palace, according to *Star* diarist Peter Tory, who in August 1985 recorded the following exchange:

Guest: You must miss Prince Andrew, Ma'am, while he is serving overseas.

The Queen: Indeed I do. Especially because he is the only one in the family who knows how to work the video.

Guest: Really ... I should have thought Prince Philip would have been able to do that.

The Queen: In that case, you have clearly never flown with my husband.

Most eventful flying career

My accolade goes to Captain Geoffrey Whittaker of St Brelade's, Jersey, who the last I heard was preparing a book on his aerial exploits, James Herriot style. Captain Whittaker's forty years of flying both with the RAF and various airlines were crowned in 1980 with one of aviation's most breathtaking landings – in a field of Devon sheep to be precise – after his Alidair Viscount had run out of fuel after being 'short-changed' in Spain. None of the sixty-two passengers or crew, nor a single sheep as it turned out, was scratched. ('We'll take good care of ewe ...')

It was only one incident in a quite incredible career. Among other stories, Captain Whittaker told me the following: 'As a pilot with an airline based on an offshore island, and a dog-lover, I was often called on by members of the Dog Club to either collect new puppies or, as on this occasion, to take a golden retriever bitch for mating. At Gatwick, having parked the aircraft for night stop, I was

walking the dog along the finger as an American
aircraft was being loaded. One of the American passengers called out, 'Hey buddy, is that your co-pilot?'
Summoning up my most dignified English accent I
replied as haughtily as I could, 'Certainly not, it's
my guide dog,' as I walked by.'

Germaine Greer

Feminist author and academic

Favourite airline
TWA (but only outside the USA). Because when
no other airline would fly me from Bangkok to
Bombay during the Indo-Pak War of 1971, they
flew as usual, only landing in a *complete* blackout
– very thrilling.

Least favourite airline
My opinion of airlines is directly related to *legroom*
– the truly important factor is the seating
configuration. Gay men make better stewards for
women than other women but Qantas'
configuration is *the pits*.

Craziest experience
The first trip I ever had in a plane from Sydney to
LHR. The Sudanese ambassador to India got on
my flight at Delhi – he was going home to *big
trouble*. He kept pouring his duty-free Scotch into
my gin and put his hands under my blanket! He
finished his journey in chains, pour soul. Not my
fault but the cabin staff took a dim view.

Costliest-ever rest stop

A sudden call of nature cost Swiss pilot Heinz Peter some £50,000. Heinz was flying a private plane from Amsterdam to Basle in October 1985 when he decided to put down at Strasbourg, France, for some natural relief. After leaping from the cockpit and demanding the way to the loo, customs officers stepped aboard and seized £20,000 of diamonds.

Heinz was furious and took the French officials to court. But they upheld their forfeiture – and, to add insult to injury, fined him another £30,000.

The one question everybody wanted to ask

When King George V received non-stop Atlantic flyer Charles Lindbergh at Buckingham Palace in 1927, he had just one question about the great aviator's marathon solo thirty-three-hour voyage.

'Now tell me, Captain Lindbergh,' he said. 'There is one thing I long to know. How did you pee?'

Most tasteless practical joke by a pilot

Passengers broke into a sweat when the captain of a transatlantic 747 came through on the intercom and asked: 'Will any good drivers aboard make themselves known to me?'

A few minutes later some began praying when he sauntered down from the flight deck carrying two long pieces of string attached to instruments on the control panel. He handed these over to an astonished passenger and said, 'Take over, will you. I've got to go to the toilet.'

He then disappeared, trying as best he could to keep a straight face, leaving the plane, thankfully for all concerned, on automatic pilot.

Four more favourite pilot japes

1. The captain emerged from the flight deck of the Trident on its way to Nice, nodded at the passengers and called to his co-pilot, 'Are you all right, John?' He then winked, hung an L-plate on the door and disappeared inside again.

2. When BEA pilots were issued with a directive telling them they should 'do their best to entertain the passengers in flight' one pilot took the instruction literally . . . he appeared suddenly in mid-flight with a ukelele and regaled the passengers with 'Swanee', 'Sonny Boy' and 'Dixie' in a deep Southern baritone.

3. It's an old favourite. In the departure hall the pilot wanders up and down the check-in queue with his head buried in a book titled *Elementary Flying Techniques*.

4. One pilot emerged from the flight deck and told astonished passengers, 'We need a navigator. Anybody help? If you've done any car rallying, that will do.' A volunteer emerged saying, 'I've been on a treasure hunt,' went up front and sat down at the navigator's seat. The flight-deck door closed and the plane then took off, passengers grasping their seats with fear. They needn't have worried about the car rallier. He was, of course, the plane's appointed navigator in plain clothes.

Dick Francis

Leading author

Best airline
Air New Zealand. My wife and I flew from Los
Angeles to Sydney with them in 1975, and the
service was absolutely first-class.

Most memorable flight
Being allowed to sit on the jump seat on the flight
deck of Concorde, both during take-off from Dubai
and landing at Heathrow during a trip from
Singapore to London early in 1980. A fantastic
trip all round.

Corniest pilot joke

It was the little old lady's first-ever flight, and as
a thunderstorm raged outside and the plane was
buffeted by turbulence, she suddenly became very
nervous.

'I'll get down, won't I?' she asked the pilot.

'Don't worry, madam, I've not left anybody up
here yet,' he replied.

Most highly publicized flying career

Plane crazy Gary Numan, son of a British Airways
worker turned pop star, spent £175,000 of his recording fortune on two headline-grabbing round-the-
world flights in 1981 and 1982. But instead of a

world-record-breaking aviator he became known as 'that publicity-seeking nutcase' and 'the pop star who smashes up aeroplanes'.

After Mr Numan hit the big time in 1981, kitting himself out with helicopter flying gloves and a 'Biggles' T-shirt, he bought no less than three planes, two Cessnas and a Piper Navajo, then decided to fly to fifty destinations in twenty countries, all in six weeks. His mother played a major part, however, phoning round all the newspapers 'just to keep people informed'.

Thanks to Mum, a series of sensational stories hit the front pages:

* How Gary was forced to crash-land at a remote Indian military airport, was arrested as a spy, and put under house arrest.

* How he collapsed at the joystick during a flight between Adelaide and Perth 'losing the use of both his arms and legs' ... Luckily his co-pilot landed the aircraft safely.

* How his plane became stranded at a remote Arctic airstrip after it developed an oil leak.

Naturally the press came round to being a little sceptical, and by far his worst moment came when he triumphantly arrived back at London's Heathrow Airport on New Year's Eve ... and not a single journalist or photographer was there to meet him.

But he was not to be robbed of his glory ... or publicity. Three weeks later his plane made an emergency landing at RAF Odiham in Hants. Well, not much coverage there. The *pièce de résistance* came, however, only a month afterwards when another light plane in which he was travelling made a crash-landing on the A3051 near Southampton.

This even made the front page of *The Times*, though the woman motorist forced to a sudden stop by Mr Numan's plummeting plane was reported to have no concern as to whether any one was injured. (She must have read the earlier stories.) Instead, she gave him a severe ticking off for obstructing the highway, before swerving round the plane and angrily driving off.

Two favourite flight-deck japes on new stewardesses

1. *The sick bag trick*. The pilot feigns illness, clutches his throat and asks the new girl for a sick bag. When she brings it she is waved away with the warning that nature is about to take its course. What actually happens is that the pilot pours vegetable soup into the bag. When she returns he professes to be much better – and is seen eating heartily from the bag with a spoon.

2. *The manual flushing trick*. To encourage bodily contact with a new girl recruit, the captain will tell her with grave concern that there is a lavatory system malfunction and 'manual flushing' is required. The girl is then asked to spread herself across the pilot's body to reach a far-off button, which she must hold down for forty-five seconds. Clothes somewhat disarranged, she is then asked to repeat the process at regular twenty-minute intervals.

(Allegedly a survey of American air hostesses who have fallen for this one showed that 20 per cent complained to their senior stewardess, 10 per cent failed to appear, 30 per cent did exactly as instructed and reappeared at intervals, and 40 per cent asked if they could come back and do it every ten minutes instead of twenty.)

Most unusual conversation between a pilot and co-pilot

Captain Geoffrey Whittaker tells me this story from his time in the RAF: 'For a ground tour I was posted to Calshot for air-traffic-control duties. One day a request came from a small unit stationed there flying Sunderlands. Did we have a spare pilot who could act as co-pilot for a seven-hour exercise with submarines? Yes, we did, and off I went.

'We had been airborne about three hours when the captain was called to lunch in the ward room; he briefed me to maintain height at 1500 feet, constant speed and fly the courses called for by the tactical navigator. Fine. As all pilots know, all aircraft are the same once in the air.

'After a few minutes a naval lieutenant with a sub. insignia on his sleeve slid into the co-pilot's seat. After gazing at the sea for a while he started looking around the cockpit, then came the first question: "What was that lever for?"

'Answer from me: "Sorry, don't know." This brought a slightly quizzical look to his face. Next, "What was that instrument for?" My answer of "Don't know" increased the quizzical expression.

' "Well," said he, "what is that switch for?" A look of disbelief crossed his face when again I answered, "Don't know."

' "Why don't you know?" was his demand. "Well," said I, "I've never actually flown one of these before."

'His exit from the flight deck was, without doubt, the fastest I have ever witnessed.'

79

Barry Norman

Leading TV presenter and film critic

Favourite airline
British Caledonian: service, courtesy and they try
harder. (And I reached that conclusion *before* I
started choosing their in-flight films!)

Least favourite
Aeroflot. They served greasy roast chicken for
breakfast at 8.30 a.m. Several greedy Russians
and Chinese were, I'm happy to say, sick.

Three things never to say to a pilot on his in-flight rounds

1. 'Who's driving?'

2. 'Have you passed your test yet?'

3. 'It must be an easy job yours, £50,000 a year for talking to the passengers while some other poor ***-ger flies the plane.'

Six most inventive uses of the plane's intercom

1. 'This is your captain speaking. We shall shortly be landing in Syria, so please fasten your seatbelts – and put back your watches 100 years.' Unidentified pilot.

2. 'Owing to heavy fog at Kennedy Airport we will now be landing in Cuba.' Pilot taking peace delegates to the United Nations.

3. 'This is your captain speaking. We are now approaching Russian airspace so I must warn you you have only thirty-five minutes of freedom left.' British Airways captain on a flight to Moscow.

4. 'Good afternoon. This is your captain speaking. Zzzz ... Zzzz ... Zzzz ...' Unidentified captain feigning he was asleep (the plane was, of course, on automatic pilot).

5. 'We're just going down to have a look at the scenery.' Jumbo jet captain 30,000 feet over the Swiss Alps who then lurched his plane downwards to the consternation of those aboard. Gin and tonics were sent flying as the plane levelled and the captain came on again to announce: 'Not to worry. Just my little joke ...'

6. 'You Catholic bastards, stop the rosary.' Aer Lingus pilot flying pilgrims to Lourdes, September 1984. He told an inquiry he was joking with his crew and didn't realize the intercom was switched on.

Quickest-thinking co-pilot

A thirty-five-year-old woman nearly caused her chartered plane to crash over Washington, DC, when, soon after take-off for Palm Beach, Florida, she made a vicious attack on the pilot, punching him on the head.

She then screamed at the co-pilot, 'Do you love me?' Thinking swiftly he replied, 'Of course I do, darling,' clutching her towards him in a warm embrace. According to airline officials, he then allowed himself to be 'alternately kissed and mauled' by the deranged woman while the pilot brought the jet down safely.

Most unusual sexual technique employed by an airline captain

Stewardess Rachel James, in her book *Coffee, Tea or Me?* (Corgi, 1971), insisted this story was true. She had been persuaded, she said, to stay with a particularly good-looking captain in Detroit. Back in his room, while he went to the lavatory and lowered his undercarriage, she slipped between the sheets.

'OK. So I'm in bed and all of a sudden the john door opens and out he comes, not a stitch on, and he's got his arms out at his sides, like wings on an airplane. And he starts running around the room and dipping from side to side and making motor sounds, like, *Rrrrrrrrrrr*.

'I swear he was nuts. All over that damn room. Then all of a sudden he zoomed at the bed, *Rrrrrrrrrr* and he said: 'OK baby! Maybe you've had it from the best. But you've never been screwed by a 707.'

Young Rachel then told how she made her excuses and made a quite noiseless exit.

First pilot to stop and ask directions

A helicopter pilot who became lost in Cornwall had a brainwave. He dropped down to fifteen feet and asked a policeman the way. Stanley Booth-Russell of Guernsey was fined £300 by Plymouth magistrates in July 1985 after the court heard how shoppers, thinking they were about to become victims of an air attack, had scattered in fear.

Best in-flight Australianism

During a night flight to Sydney the Australian captain inadvertently left the intercom to the passenger cabin switched on. As the Antipodean coast thrust into view, the pilot was heard loudly to remark: 'What I need most right now is a hot Sheila and an ice-cold beer.'

The stewardess rushed from the rear of the plane to warn the pilot of his 'own goal'. Seeing her sprinting towards the cockpit, one of the passengers shouted: 'Don't forget his ice-cold beer.'

I'm Randy, Fly Me

No other profession has provoked so much fantasizing – or featured in so much advertising – as that of the air stewardess.

To the girls themselves, well, apart from trying to escape the greasy paws of every inebriated male groper who ever flew, they're just trying to be of service . . .

One caring stewardess washed a passenger's shirt after he spilled red wine down it. This she accomplished successfully and popped it in to the microwave to dry. The passenger was delighted with the immaculately clean shirt except for one small thing – the microwave had melted all the buttons.

The passenger grabbed the British Airways stewardess's hat, garnished it with salt and pepper . . . and ate it. The stewardess remembered her training. She smiled and told him sweetly: 'I hope you enjoyed your lunch, sir.'

Let's hear it for the air girls . . .

Best air stewardess memory

The story goes that one girl was being harassed by two persistent would-be Lotharios at opposite ends of the plane. One Romeo was determined to get the girl to visit his apartment. The other was determined to get an invitation to visit *hers*. Finally, when she just about wished she could scream, she took the key from passenger No. 1, carefully wrote his address on it, and put it in her pocket faithfully promising to be there the moment she had cleared the airport formalities. Back with passenger No. 2 she dug out the key and address from her pocket, gave it him and whispered, 'Come up just as soon as you can.'

Most bizarre complication arising from a plane cancellation

A sexy British Airways stewardess was rather distraught when her flight home to London from Paris was cancelled, reported the Heathrow Airport staff magazine *Skyport*. For she had left her 'kinky' husband bound and naked in a wardrobe. The stewardess had strapped him and left him dangling from the cupboard rails before leaving for her six-hour round trip to Paris – just the thing to keep him from getting up to any mischief, you might have thought.

But the full horror dawned when the plane broke down and the girl was not happy to leave her bonded goods all night – being tied up, he could hardly answer the phone. Instead she called Scotland Yard with an urgent request for police to break into their London home, unfasten him, and ease him gently down to the ground. There were no charges, although it is said the husband did ask ... if he could be bound over for the next twelve months.

Fastest stewardess love match

Stewardess Sue Fan had certainly made an impression on the long flight to the Far East. So much so that one of her passengers, wealthy Arizona farmer Jim Bates, grabbed her, kissed her, and proposed to her almost in one breath. But she told him he must wait for an answer as he went off to change flights at Hong Kong's Kai-tak Airport.

Almost immediately she changed her mind. She sent a message through another stewardess saying she would marry him after all. Back came the reply from another stewardess, Dorothy Cooper: 'Your message passed on, but he has already proposed to me and I have accepted.'

Roy Kinnear

Actor/comedian

Craziest flight
On a flight from the Bahamas to Heathrow, I was allowed to sit on the flight deck as the plane came in to land. At the vital moment that landing lights should have been visible, nothing could be seen. The pilot, co-pilot, and engineer, together with three stewardesses, all had their noses pressed up to the windscreen and it was a stewardess who spotted them away over to the left. I was the only white-faced passenger who knew why the plane swerved so steeply just before landing.

World's steamiest air girls

One airline decided to make its image a little racier in the early 1970s by dreaming up the idea of the hostesses who literally 'took off' with the aircraft.

The girls were paid £200 a month extra by Southwest Airlines of Texas to shed their dresses in specially designed 'love flights'. The scene-setting to soothe furrowed male brows included the wearing of hot pants and skimpy sweaters with the offer of a special 'love punch' in ice-chilled glasses. The plan was grounded by other airlines when a warning was issued about possible mile-high heart attacks by overexcited businessmen.

World's sexiest stewardesses

These were undoubtedly the eight girls who were fired by 'The Smiling Airline', Air Zimbabwe in July 1983. The stewardesses, all single, had obviously done too much smiling. All eight had become pregnant.

Announcing the sackings, Transport Minister Farai Masango said he was 'alarmed' by the pregnancy rate since white stewardesses gave way to blacks in 1980. The rights of transfer to another job of mothers-to-be had been 'grossly abused', he remarked. 'Many stewardesses seem to think there is an open season for pregnancies at Air Zimbabwe.'

Well, serves them right for introducing 'club class'.

The stewardesses' worst critic

I didn't say it girls, but, according to acid wit Joan Rivers, 'You're all tramps.' Here are the worst of her anti-hostess barbs:

* *They marry rich* ... They get married because they don't wear underwear and the men go bananas. They keep saying to men 'let me get you a blanket' and climb on up ... Sit by the window you see the earth. Sit by the aisle and you see the moon.

* *Aren't they bitchy to women* ... 'Stewardess, my window is open,' – 'Not my aisle.' 'Stewardess, where's my seat?' – 'Three inches below where it was last year.' I got sick in the plane. 'Stewardess, I need a throw-up bag.' – 'Doesn't your dress have pockets?'

* *They're all tramps.* Never let a stewardess go
with your husband. 'Stewardess, my husband's
cold.' – 'He wasn't last night.' And the men love
them. 'Welcome aboard, welcome aboard.' Wake
'em up in the middle of the night and what do
they say? 'Welcome aboard, welcome aboard.'

(This extract from Miss Rivers' stage act can be
heard on her Geffen/CBS LP 'Can We Talk' – in the
UK GEF 25676, London, 1983.)

Four things never to do when trying to chat up an air hostess

Penny Sutton (real name Clare Russell of Chiswick)
wrote a book in 1973 called *The Stewardesses*
(Sphere), which she said was based on a diary of her
exploits aloft. In the book she gives the following
tips on how to go about dating a hostess:

1. Don't show her pictures of your children, wife,
dog, pet nannygoat, etc., and tell her how much you
miss them. Chances are that she will start missing
them, too, so that by the time you get around to the
'I'm so lonely without Mabel and the kids, how about
sharing a pizza with me to stop me committing
suicide' bit she will feel like she is betraying everybody right down to the nannygoat before she takes
one bite. She will also feel that you are a teeny bit
wet.

2. Don't say: 'Er, excuse me but I – er, don't know
my way around this town and I – er want to buy –
er, my wife some perfume and I – er, was wondering
if you could – er, help me, and – er have dinnerandg-
otobedwithme!' The last bit comes out in a rush and

you wonder why he had to drop the commercial into such a lousy programme slot.

3.   Don't avoid her eyes as you leave the plane but shove a note into her hand which says 'Jack Sprat. Ring me Plaza Hotel 18.30'. Big deal! Why should any girl want to ring you when you don't have the guts to say hello to her when you've got the chance!

4.   Don't try to grab her just when she is rushing past you delicately balancing four dirty food trays or worse still dangling a 'puking baby'.

'All you have to do,' says Penny, 'is to wait for the right moment, look her straight in the eye and say: 'I would very much like to have dinner with you tonight, are you free?' (The answer will invariably be no, but at least you gave it a go.)

AUTHOR'S NOTE: I suppose the same rules apply to stewards, but I've never tried.

Worst-ever air-hostess bust-up

When an American airliner lost cabin pressure over Los Angeles in February 1967, one of the stewardesses suffered worse than most. Her inflatable bra expanded to an ungovernable forty-four inches and brought her to a near panic. The larger-than-life problem was resolved, however, when she managed a sudden let-down, puncturing her ballooning figure with a hairpin.

Most costly anatomy lesson

In August 1975 Senator William Proxmire gave one of his celebrated 'Golden Fleece Awards' to the Federal Aviation Authority for a $50,000 investigation into the body measurements of airline stewardesses. The study of 423 girls training at an academy in Fort Worth, Texas, resulted in a 109-page report detailing seventy-nine measurements from head to toe of each girl. The idea was to aid in the design of safety equipment. Included in the measurements were such mind boggling metrics as: 'Knee to knee breadth while sitting', 'the skinfold of the upper arm and the posterior calf', 'the height of the nose' and 'the popliteal length of the buttocks'. (Now there's a real chat-up line to try on a stewardess: 'I'd like to measure the popliteal length of your buttocks.' No, please don't say I've told you to try it.)

Jeremy Child

Actor and baronet

Favourite airline
TWA. They're fun. A lot of trips to LA and back.

Least favourite airline
British Airways. The food is filthy.

Most bizarre happening aloft
A relative getting stuck in the loo with a fat lover whilst attempting to join the Mile High Club. This is *true!*

Most embarrassing moment
On a recent Air Canada flight from Montreal, I was accused of being Paul Eddington from 'Yes Minister'.

Most surprising extra passenger

Blonde Gulf Air stewardess Susan Mackie from Aberdeen, Scotland, had an unexpected surprise during a one-night stopover in Doha, Qatar, in August 1984. She gave birth to a 6lb baby boy. Susan said she first thought she had caught a stomach bug, but then managed to deliver the baby herself in her hotel room. Medical experts agreed it would be possible for a woman who travelled regularly by air to have a 'very irregular' menstrual cycle and possibly not realize she was pregnant. 'It was a complete surprise. I had no idea I was pregnant,' said new mum Susan on arrival at London's Heathrow Airport.

For your discomfort and inconvenience ... a dozen ways stewardesses get revenge on a passenger they take a dislike to

Make sure you're nice to the cabin staff ... They have ways of making you suffer ...

1. *The cold shoulder.* That skilful deaf ear and brusque brush past when Wilbur hollers 'Hey, miss!' to no avail.

2. *The non-alcoholic drink.* When Wilbur asks for 'another large one' all he's likely to get is another mixer. (This was rumbled by one leading pop star who rounded on a stewardess and asked, very politely: 'Please, this time, could I have a little Scotch in my Scotch?')

3. *The food or drink spill.* A favourite, though some stewardesses are wary that Wilbur might ask

them to clean it up (some men actually lob precious alcohol on to their trousers to get a hostess to bend over them). The traditional response here is to get a male steward to 'camp it up', mincing towards them limp-wristedly asking: 'Is it you who wants the clean-up, duckie?'

4. *The check-in girl's revenge.* Wilbur has to be at his most debonair at the check-in desk. (If he isn't, he's a fool.) If he's impolite, he'll find himself seated next to a howling infant, by the lavatory (hell on night flights) or in between a raddled hippie and an Oriental stoker going back home, both in clothes they haven't changed for six months.

5. *The buckle in the groin.* This requires practised timing. The metal seat-strap buckle is pulled out, and deftly allowed to spring back (twang!) with maximum force into the parts of Wilbur which when struck hurt him the most.

6. *The white-hot flannel.* If Wilbur makes a bad impression right away he is likely to have a grossly superheated flannel flung into his face.

7. *The overcooked meal.* Some airline meals are bad enough – but an extra two minutes under the microwave and *yuk*.

8. *The fake frightener.* The stewardess adopts a terror-stricken look while staring Wilbur straight in the face. She then exclaims: 'My God, I think we're going down,' before rushing to the back of the plane, feigning shock.

9. *Petty cash.* Wilbur is told unsympathetically he can have change for his drinks only in the currency of the country he has just left.

10. *The rollerball trolley.* Wilbur will find how, by some strange coincidence, every time the trolley

comes near him it will bump savagely into his thigh or feet, especially while he is asleep.

11 *Time, gentlemen, please.* Thirsty Wilbur will be left last to be served from the duty-free trolley ... and when it comes to his turn, told: 'Sorry, sir, customs regulations require that our duty-free stocks now be sealed.'

12. *The finger of fate.* Worst of all, a vengeful air girl can 'finger' Wilbur as the plane docks, telling ground staff he is a suspected smuggler. He will then face an hour or more of strip-search and interrogation. So Wilbur, be good to them all! Then you'll really 'have a nice day'.

Every steward and stewardess's favourite rude passenger story (1)

One troublesome lady passenger had asked a stewardess for everything ... Finally her 101st request was, 'Have you got anything for a sore throat.' The long-suffering stewardess sauntered back to the galley and brought back on a tray a carving knife.

Every steward and stewardess's favourite rude passenger story (2)

It has been told apocryphally many times, but really happened to a Gulf Air steward on a flight to Bahrain in 1981 ...

The woman passenger in first-class had been demanding every attention from the cabin staff. So when her baby filled its nappy, she rang the bell for the steward. 'Here, change it!' she demanded.

'Certainly, madam,' said the steward, happily

taking off the wet infant and returning to dump in her lap ... another baby, with the rejoinder, 'Will this one do?'

The steward was suspended after an inquiry. OK, he was harassed, said a colleague – but he could have given her a better swap.

Worst-ever stewardess joke

My nomination comes from Frank Sinatra: 'You know you're travelling faster than sound on Concorde when the stewardess slaps your face before you've said what you're thinking.'

Best-ever stewardess joke

The Catholic priest and the Seventh Day Adventist minister were sitting next to each other on a flight. The priest ordered a Scotch and water. The minister said, 'I'd rather commit adultery than drink.'

The priest called back the stewardess and said, 'Take this back please, miss, I didn't know we were allowed a choice.'

High Flyers

Curt Smith, half of the Tears for Fears pop duo, while in America in the middle of a world tour in August 1985, spent £1800 on a return Concorde trip to London so he could go for a quick spin in his wife's car. He wanted to celebrate the end of a year's driving ban.

Not a lot of people know this, but one weekend, Michael Caine flew 6000 miles from London to Hollywood and then back to location in Majorca. He did it just to end his relationship with then girl-friend Camilla Sparv.

And, I know he's an odd size, but Prince Rainier has been known to fly to London from Monaco 'just to buy a couple of suits'. Yes, celebrities have always been known to go to extremities in the air . . .

Craziest reason for crossing the atlantic

At Orly Airport in Paris, actress Shirley Maclaine got into a deep conversation on transcendental mysticism, yoga and Buddhism with a friend she was seeing off to the United States. Suddenly the flight to New York was called. 'Don't let that inter-rupt our talk,' Shirley told her buddy. 'Let's catch the plane.' 'But you're not going to New York,' said the astonished friend. 'It'll be worth it just for the chat,' said Miss Maclaine, who flew back to Paris the next day, the chat with her friend having cost a cool $1000.

Craziest trip to the dentist's by an actress who later starred in 'Dynasty'

A passion for flying got sultry actress Joan Collins suspended more than once from star roles. In 1960, filming in Italy, she got toothache . . . and decided to go and see her dentist in New York. That, at least, was her story, though it must be pointed out that Warren Beatty, her beau at that time, was there and she did manage to look him up while getting her tooth drilled. Joan then made the round trip to New York four times in eight weeks, at a cost of £400 a trip. Her reward was not the hand of Mr Beatty but suspension three times from the set of *Esther and the King*. Then her contract with Twentieth Century Fox ended, and she missed the chance to star in *Cleopatra*. You'll remember that Elizabeth Taylor got the part. High-flying Joan said at the time: 'I have always lived life out of a suitcase.'

More amazing celebrity air jaunts

Others among the great, good and famous who have used aeroplanes as you or I might use a cab . . .

1. When tempestuous French actor *Jean-Paul Belmondo* was making *The Blue Max* in Paris, he flew every evening to Dublin to be with his then girlfriend Ursula Andress, who was filming in Ireland. He caught a plane back to Paris each morning.

2. *Shirley Maclaine* commuted regularly from Los Angeles for weekends in Tokyo in the 1960s – at $1500 a time – where husband Steve Parker was working as a leading film producer. She said, 'If I'm filming in Hollywood I get on the plane after shooting on Friday night, and I'm in Tokyo in sixteen hours. I read a couple of books or catch up with my sleep in the jet. I come back Monday.'

3. *Mia Farrow* wanted her hair done and could not spare the time to fly from Hollywood to London to her stylist Vidal Sassoon. So she sent tickets for Mr Sassoon to fly out to Los Angeles.

4. *The Duchess of Windsor* went one better, flying both her New York hairdresser *and* his assistant out to the Bahamas when she was holidaying there.

5. *Princess Lee Radziwill* flew an interior decorator 2400 miles from Milan just to tell her what wallpaper to choose to decorate a Chinese room at her country home at Henley.

5. *Leslie Caron* flew regularly to Paris to choose furniture for her London home.

7. *Princess Ira Furstenburg* lived in Rome, but insisted on buying all her clothes in Paris.

8. *Marlene Dietrich* used to fly from the United States to Italy to her shoemakers Ferragamo. (She used to buy more than 100 pairs a year this way, insisting never to appear in public wearing the same shoes twice.)

9. *George Hamilton* had his barber, Art Windsor, flown 6462 miles from Los Angeles to Shepperton Studios, England, and back while he was making *The Victors*.

10 British actress *Moira Lister* once flew from London to Paris to change a cookery book. The

recipes were in French and she couldn't work out
the metric measures. (It wasn't her only impromptu
dash across the Channel. She once landed at Paris
without her passport. Undaunted, she flew back to
London to collect it, then caught the next plane back
to the French capital.)

Sandor Elès

Paul Ross of ITV's 'Crossroads'

Favourite airline
Austrian Airlines. Because the stewardesses are so
charming and because it is a small airline. Once
on a trip to London, they held up the whole
aeroplane for ten minutes just for me after I
checked in at the wrong gate. What service!

Least favourite
Air Maroc. The only airline I ever travelled on that
was a whole day late!

Most unusual experience
Once on a trip to Helsinki I sat next to Marlene
Dietrich. She chatted all the way there, but never
introduced herself. I purposely avoided asking
about her legendary self. But towards landing-
time I confessed that I was an actor, on my way to
make a film with John Huston. She became
heated: 'I am Mrs Martha M. Schlogenberger, a
florist from New York and when you see that
sonofabitch, tell him to pay for the flowers I sent
for him five years ago!'

Most inconvenient airline superstition

Alana Stewart told her husband George Hamilton in June 1975 that he must on no account have anything to do with a plane connected with the number seven. Difficult, as poor George, who was trying to fly from New York to Los Angeles at the time explained: 'The only flights out were on 707s or 747s and flights with seven in the number or landing at seven. You know what? I had to hang around for two whole days waiting to get out of town.'

Another time she told 'Gorgeous' George that due to a premonition he must sit in seat 8B on a tourist flight to New York. 'So I did,' said George, 'and found myself sitting between a drunken man and his wife who wanted to be together and were furious with me for refusing to move. We almost came to blows. How could I tell them I had to sit there because I was going to be the only surviving passenger on the plane?

'Even the captain came back and asked me to move. After going through all that, when we finally landed and the plane hadn't crashed I was *furious*.'

Most lovelorn celebrity charter

Jerry Hall tells in her book *Tall Tales* (Elm Tree, 1985) how she adventurously chartered a plane to be reunited with boyfriend Mick Jagger, who was sailing up the Amazon for a film and had written to her saying he was lonely. 'I had no plans, no money, but I knew what I wanted!' said Jerry lustfully. Using just high charm and the instruction 'Big boat, Big boat!' our heroine managed to find our hero, with the aid of an old plane which landed in a clearing, South American Indians ('Real Indians all painted with loincloths and stuff'), and a canoe.

'To see his face light up when he saw me ... he was so shocked. And he came running and grabbed me out of the canoe ... it was exactly like a scene out of a movie ...' Everyone was amazed, said Jerry. Mick had arrived after a long boat journey and three nights camping out, and a seaplane bringing others had crashed into the jungle.

The lovers subsequently spent an enraptured two weeks in a monsoon sleeping under 'a piece of mildewed black plastic'. The film Mr Jagger had been making was never completed. *Plane Crazy*.

Unhappiest co-passengers

It wasn't exactly a Stairway to Heaven when rock stars Robert Plant and Jimmy Page met Kojak hulk Telly Savalas on a transatlantic jet. The two sides travelled on the same plane from Los Angeles to London and to say they didn't hit the right notes ... well Mr Savalas refused to give details of the verbal fisticuffs on the flight, saying only: 'They're just a drunken group who flipped out.' But a spokesman for the Led Zeppelin group (no jokes about high musicians, please) shouted to photographers: 'Come back and take pictures of us – we're more famous than him.' Later at his hotel, Kojak shot from the hip: 'Somebody can be rude to me once or maybe twice, but nobody three times ...' Who hates ya, baby!

Worst in-flight joke by a movie star

Hollywood star Marlon Brando was ordered off a National Airlines jet at Los Angeles Airport when on boarding he asked, 'Is this flight for Cuba?' The stewardess had not recognized Brando, who was travelling incognito in beard and pigtails, and she complained to the pilot. He ordered 'the sloppily dressed passenger' to leave the plane. A National

---

David Steel

Leader of the Liberal Party

Favourite airline
Lofteidir/Icelandair. It gives excellent and polite service.

Least favourite
Sabena. They say the letters stand for 'Such A Bloody Experience – Never Again.' The food is awful and the last time I travelled back from Brussels they cancelled a service and combined two flights with no apology or notice.

Favourite air story
An argument over whether tea or coffee was the drink being served was resolved when it was discovered the pot contained one tea bag and one coffee bag!

Airlines spokesman said the airline had been hit harder than most by a spate of hijackings, one plane being forced to go to Havana less than twenty-four hours before. Perhaps Brando should have made them an offer they couldn't refuse.

Most uncomfortable VIP flight

Sir Alec Guinness was making his first transatlantic flight to star in a Hollywood film. But over Iceland the bunk in his Scandinavian Airways jet collapsed. Sir Alec, star of *Kind Hearts and Coronets*, did not betray his calling as the archetypal stiff-upper-lip Englishman. Finding himself hanging head down, with his legs suspended in mid-air, Sir Alec stoically remained exactly where he was. He said, 'I was so afraid of disturbing other passengers, especially a rather irate lady in the next berth, that I stayed in that position all night.'

Most boring Royal flight

Veteran Buckingham Palace aviator Prince Philip was greeted by a reception committee as he disembarked from the Royal jet. The chairman asked him politely, 'How was your flight?'

'Have you ever flown in a plane,' the Prince asked icily.

'Yes, your Royal Highness, often.'

'Well it was just like that,' was the unkind reply.

Mightiest put-down of flying

Opening the new £200 million Terminal 4 at Heathrow in April, 1986, Prince Charles gave his verdict on the down-side of flying. He said his ninety-minute tour of the airport terminal had left him footsore, and suggested it was all a conspiracy by the airline industry. 'My wife and I have walked miles. I have come to the conclusion that the distances that passengers or prospective passengers have to march through terminals is designed to ensure that when you climb into the aircraft you are so exhausted that you fall asleep instantly and feel no pain for the rest of the journey.' Offered a chair to enable her to sign the visitors' book Princess Diana echoed her husband's view. 'It's nice to sit down,' she sighed.

Worst case of a rock star throwing his weight around

Mick Jagger wins this award for his ungallant treatment of hostess Pauline Lough while waiting to take off from London on a Pan Am 747 in December 1971. After a blazing row in the first-class cabin of Flight PA121, Jagger allegedly rushed at Miss Lough from behind, pulled her backwards by the arm, and said: 'You talk to me like that again and I'll kick you up your ****.'

Miss Lough had told how, at the request of the purser, she had asked the Rolling Stone and his entourage of nine to change places after they had pushed past other passengers and commandeered the wrong first-class seats. Jagger told her, 'Shut up, we've a long way to go,' she reported.

'I told him that other passengers whose seats they had taken also had a long way to go,' said Pauline. 'He got abusive and swore at me.'

There followed the incident in the aisle when Jagger is alleged to have grabbed her, in full view of disapproving passengers, including a titled lady.

On arrival in LA, Jagger denied touching her, though remained unchivalrous to the last. He said, 'I'd like to have given her a good slap in the face.' Well, I suppose that's better than a kick up the ****.

Cheapest way to travel first class

Not all VIPs and celebrities go first. Many think it's far too expensive. Or too boring – full of business types. Some travel economy safe in the knowledge they'll be spotted, feted, and upgraded by the cabin staff. On one voyage in 1983, Jackie Onassis, conservatively valued at £25 million, was returning 'steerage' from China with her half-brother Jamie Auchincloss and their uncle. There was a seat available for her in first class the stewardess rushed to inform her, but not, unfortunately, for her companions. 'Don't trouble,' said Jackie, gathering up her luggage and making for the first-class cabin with the cheery farewell to her family: 'See you in New York.'

Christopher Martin-Jenkins

Cricket author, writer and commentator

Best airline
Singapore Airlines, remembering a journey from India to Australia when the hot flannels and pretty stewardesses were like manna from heaven after an exhausting cricket tour.

Craziest journey
I once travelled with the Welsh sports commentator Alun Williams to a BBC meeting in

Worst case of VIP down-grading

Earl Mountbatten of Burma flew from the United States to England in November 1970 in the cargo hold of a Pan Am Boeing 707. Keen to keep a dinner engagement in London with King Gustaf of Sweden after dining in Washington with President Nixon, Earl Mountbatten found the scheduled passenger service arrived too late. So he promptly downgraded himself to cargo and travelled in the hold, surrounded by sundry crates and parcels. Said Lord Louis afterwards: 'It was a marvellous trip.' Opposition leader Edward Heath repeated the feat in 1975, becoming the first ex-prime minister to send himself air freight.

Belfast, due to start at 10 a.m. Delayed start due to fog. Over Belfast, more fog. Pilot (Irish, casual voice) kept saying: 'We'll just nip below the fog to see if we can see the runway' – a steep descent and then a swift ascent – followed by 'We'll give it a few minutes and then have another go'. We finally got down at the fifth attempt and Alun and I arrived at the meeting at 5 p.m. just as the chairman was saying, 'I think that settles it then, gentlemen – now who would like a drink?'

Most bizarre experience
I was once held up at Bombay Airport when an airport vehicle – really – crashed into the gangplank!

Best act of celebrity heroism

Comedian Freddie Starr's audience was already hysterical when he began a very special perform-ance 20,000 feet up. Panic had set in among passen-gers on a Las Vegas bound Boeing 737 when they were unsympathetically informed that the plane's undercarriage had jammed. But Freddie decided to lift spirits by performing his comedy routine until the plane landed safely at Los Angeles. Said Freddie afterwards: 'I decided that there
was only one thing to do in
the circumstances
– my act.'

Most inconsiderate celebrity

Paul McCartney and his wife Linda were an hour late for a Qantas jumbo flight to Australia in October 1975 and hundreds of passengers had to wait, strapped into their seats, until the two VIPs appeared. McCartney and his wife, three children and backing group Wings were booked on the plane at the start of a concert tour, and staff from the recording company had beseeched Qantas to wait for them. McCartney could have soothed simmering temperatures aboard but his attitude was cool to an extreme. Why was he late? 'We overslept a little, what's the panic,' he said. His wife Linda said, 'Why were we late? Oh, the eggs wouldn't boil?'

Worst tantrum at the check-in

Leaving on Concorde for New York in March 1983, actor Richard Harris threw what is euphemistically described as 'a wobbly' after being charged £210 in excess baggage to get his eleven pieces of luggage aboard. Joan Collins had just made a series of advertisements in return for free travel for BA, and Mr Harris reacted by screaming, 'If I had tits like that they would let me fly for nothing.' Harris aged fifty-two, undiplomatically wearing a flying suit with an Air France pilot's badge said, 'I keep the flag flying too. People like me keep Concorde in the air. I've travelled ten times on the thing this year and I've never been charged excess baggage.' British Airways denied that female appendages had anything to do with it. They said of Miss Collins: 'We have the same arrangement with Omar Sharif, and he doesn't have the same, er, attributes.'

Most embarrassing in-flight drink

Gerry Fitt, MP, later Lord Fitt, leader of Northern Ireland's Catholic SDLP, found himself snookered when he was a late boarder on a flight from Belfast to London. To his embarrassment he had been seated next to the Reverend Ian Paisley, abstemious leader of Ulster's hardline Unionists. He looked round for another seat. There was none.

When the stewardess brought round the trolley, Fitt ordered a Scotch, noting the disapproval of his teetotal companion.

Fitt searched through one pocket; then another. He had joined the flight without any cash. Supreme ignominy followed when he was forced to borrow cash from Dr Paisley to purchase his tot of the 'Devil's brew'.

Most public celebrity call

The newspaper called it 'Jimmy's Little Riddle' when, in November 1985, former world motor-racing champion James Hunt disgraced himself on a British Airways 747 flying from London to Sydney by performing what was described as 'a bodily function' in the gangway. Mr Hunt had apparently been enjoying duty-free drinks when he received the call of nature and dashed for the lavatories. Alas, all were occupied so he just did what came naturally – in the plane's aisle. Fellow BBC presenter Esther Rantzen was also on the flight, but denied being splashed when the racing star sought relief. Hunt's wife Sarah said, 'He was sleepwalking and didn't know what he was doing.' A British Airways staff member quoted by the *Sun* said: 'He was incapable, not sleepwalking. I don't think he apologized

because he wasn't in any condition to say anything.'
So a riddle it remained ...

First former Defence Secretary to attempt a hijack

This dubious achievement award goes to Mr Denis Healey, who, arriving back at Heathrow Airport in the early morning after talks at the UN with Secretary-General Javier Perez de Cuellar in April 1982, tried to step into a waiting official car. Mr Healey had spied a familiar VIP 'greeter' and said: 'I suppose you're here to meet me?' Alas he was not and the 'greeter' had to block the path of the No 2 man in Jim Callaghan's government saying: 'Not for a couple of years, at least.' Outranking Mr Healey, and the man for whom the car had been sent, was, yes, couldn't you have guessed, the Senior Permanent Secretary of State for Lesotho.

Unauthorized Travel

The man who started it all with a daring dash across the tarmac (or field as it was at the time) was M. Armand Lotti, son of a hotel proprietor, who in September 1928 became the first air stowaway when he crept aboard the Canary Bird plane piloted by Assolant and Lefevre on their attempt to be the first men to fly direct from Paris to New York. M. Lotti succeeded despite the attentions of his father, who had hired private detectives and asked for police presence to stop his loony son, as he saw it, hopping aboard such a dangerous contraption. M. Lotti jr outwitted them all, managing to stow aboard the plane both for its first aborted take-off (he ran away and hid overnight in a shed) and the real thing. Sadly his bid to become the first stowaway to cross the Atlantic failed when the plane hit engine trouble and was forced to put down in North Africa.

It's a fact of aviation history that many have followed in the footsteps of the 'dotty' M. Lotti since, not all of them having the most comfortable of rides.

Youngest-ever stowaway

Three-year-old Mark Woo-Sam became the youngest-ever self-motivated stowaway when he crept aboard a TWA jumbo bound for London from Los Angeles in August 1972. He was found hiding in a lavatory twenty minutes after take-off. Mark had clambered on to the plane to be with his father, Mr James Woo-Sam, a forty-year-old psychologist from Inglewood, California. The canny three-year-old had come to the airport with his mother and two sisters to see his father off, but managed to give them the slip. Mr Woo-Sam said, 'I heard an announcement

asking for the parents of a small boy found in the toilet at the back of the aircraft to come forward. I was horrified when I saw Mark being carried down the aisle bawling his head off.' Later Mr Woo-Sam handed Mark over to two TWA 'aunties' for the flight back to Los Angeles. 'He doesn't seem in the least bit at all upset,' his father commented. 'He obviously likes flying.'

Steve Race

Broadcaster and musicologist

Craziest moment

In one of the editions of the panel game 'My Music', I asked Frank Muir which piece of music would be *least* suitable for playing to nervous air travellers. He suggested 'That Old Black Magic', which includes the line 'Down and down I go, round and round I go, in a spin . . .'

I know from recording the announcements myself for in-flight tapes that the production companies have to vet items very carefully. For example, we dropped the movement 'Mars' from Gustav Holst's suite 'The Planets' because when people have their feet off the ground they don't care to be reminded that wars occasionally break out. This being so, I was half delighted, half horrified, when a plane in which I was travelling myself took off to the dulcet strains of a song called 'Didn't We?' Perhaps only I knew the first words of the song: 'This time we almost made that long hard climb, didn't we?'

World's most uncomfortable transatlantic flight

Armando Ramirez, aged twenty-two, was the miracle stowaway who survived an eight-and-three-quarter-hour flight at altitudes of up to 36,000 feet with virtually no oxygen and temperatures as low as −40 degrees C. You don't believe it? Doctors refused to at first. They were convinced there would be at least permanent damage to his heart, liver, kidneys and brain, to name but a few. In fact, Armando left hospital with no ill effects, having braved almost a worse ordeal than his flight – virtually all of Spain's specialists queuing up to poke and prod him.

Amazing Armando had made his 4500–mile flight from Cuba huddled in the wheel bay of a DC-8 jet thundering its way from Havana to Madrid. He told how he had hidden at the end of the runway as the Iberia flight 942 had taxied for take-off, clambering on to the plane's four giant wheels at the last moment. It nearly didn't come off. When the captain tried to raise the undercarriage a red warning light flashed, indicating a fault. He lowered and raised the undercarriage again and Armando, dressed only in a light pair of trousers, a tropical shirt and one shoe – the other having fallen off – was aboard in what was surely history's most uncomfortable long-distance flight.

Most unusual urge to fly

Peter Evans, aged thirty-one, a telegraphist at London's Heathrow Airport, signed off a message abruptly and the next anyone knew he was sucking a boiled sweet aboard a Caravelle taking off for

Paris. Calmly he walked across the Orly Airport tarmac . . . and went to sleep on a bench. The stowaway was discovered and despatched back to London with a public wigging from his wife Sheila: 'Just what I won't do to him when he gets home.' But just over a month later Peter did it again. This time he decided to fly back to London by stowing away a second time. He wasn't very good at it, ending up in Rome instead. Sheila said, 'I told him if he did anything so ridiculous again, I'd be wilder than he'd ever seen me.'

So why the compulsion for stowing away? Anything to do with wild wife Sheila? Well, yes, in a way. Said Peter: 'I'm a frustrated flautist.' Frustrated *what*? 'Yes, that's right. For ten years my whole life revolved round playing the flute. Then my wife persuaded me to give up music and get a steady job. As I tap away now on the teleprinter there are times I have to get away from it all or go mad. My ambition is to conduct a first-class orchestra.'

Trilled unmoved Sheila in a crescendo: 'I'll slaughter him when he gets home.'

Best-dressed pilot

Airline engineers checking a BEA Trident for take-off from Zurich were astonished to find the captain sitting at the controls in full evening dress. Furthermore, they decided he had been enjoying himself a little too much prior to the flight. Inquiries showed that this was not, in fact, the captain, but a late-night reveller, an engineering graduate from Oxford University. The over-dressed 'captain' said he had been at the airport to see off a woman acquaintance.

The plane was withdrawn for a full security search, while our friend was given a severe 'dressing down'.

Anneka Rice

'Treasure Hunt' TV star

Favourite airline
Castle Air – the helicopter charter company we use for 'Treasure Hunt'. If I say anything else, they'll push me out during the next series!

Least favourite
I refuse to answer on the grounds that I may have to fly with them again in the next series of 'Wish You Were Here' and I don't fancy a cockroach club sandwich!

Funniest experience
On a flight back from Tel Aviv to London a particularly rude man was double-booked into my brother's seat in front of me. Even though he was in the wrong, he steadfastly refused to move and my brother was re-seated. However, as the plane started its final surge down the runway for take-off, a bottle of cherry brandy my brother had placed in the overhead locker above him, broke, sending a steady stream of sticky red liquid on to our rude friend's head and lap. A combination of g force during take-off and the seatbelt sign being firmly on, meant he was completely soaked before he was able – or allowed – to stand up. The air hostesses enjoyed it too!

Sweetest giveaway

Air hostess Gina Rossi had a surprise response when she offered a woman passenger some peppermints. *Two* pairs of hands made a dive for the dish – one from above the woman's waist, and another pair from underneath her skirt. Three-year-old Ahmed Ebrahim was one of three Bedouin stowaways whose predilection for sweets gave them away on a flight from Catania, Sicily, for Tripoli, Libya.

Most unusual reason for jet-jumping

John Thomas, a twenty-eight-year-old American (no comment on a man with a name like that) stowed away on board a Pan Am Boeing freighter leaving Frankfurt in November 1964 ... because he was determined to vote in the American presidential election. Mr J. T. hid in the lavatory for the journey, even evading detection at a refuelling stop in Brussels. However, John Thomas (I bet they didn't believe his name either) was detained in London as an illegal immigrant.

Luckily for him he was then put aboard a scheduled US service to New York. He said: 'I want to get home to vote. I am a Johnson man, I don't feel the president is going to win by a big majority. I think it will be like our last presidential election, a very close thing. I shall be voting for Bobby Kennedy who is standing against Senator Keating. Yes, I'll be home in time to register my vote.'

Mr Thomas's political judgement proved as embarrassing as his name. Johnson beat Senator Barry Goldwater by a landslide, and his one vote was *not* crucial.

Most successful bogus steward

It is a good job that few succeed in brazenly impersonating pilots, but there are many recorded instances of smart young men travelling the globe after posing as stewards. One such success story was that of trans-world conman William Cohn, who over two years fooled cabin crews into accepting him, logging visits to London, Paris, Hong Kong, Japan, Hawaii, Kenya and South Africa. No one queried the smartly dressed flight attendant who simply walked past security men at airports. Flight crews all too readily swallowed his story that he had been transferred to their plane at the last minute.

But would be steward Cohn made a crucial in-flight error. He was *nice* to passengers. Too nice, in fact, by far. He was caught when glowing commendations flew back to his 'superiors'. They tried to dig out his file to log the accolades . . . and found there wasn't one.

In December 1982, Miami police were alerted and Cohn was charged with taking more than £27,000 worth of free flights.

Longest time in the lavatory

Barry McIlwraith, aged fourteen, of Glasgow, stowed away on an airliner for Canada and suffered a little inconvenience for it, spending four hours locked in the ladies' toilet. He escaped detection for that long, but then came the inevitable hammering on the door. Well, three and a half hours, maybe, but who would spend four hours in the ladies, reasoned a quick-thinking stewardness.

Brough Scott

ITV racing commentator and journalist

Favourite Airline
Singapore Airlines . . . not just the girls – but to
make that long journey back through the
seemingly endless night needs a very gentle and
willing touch.

Least favourite airline
Czech Airways. Based on only one flight – Prague
to Budapest at 8 a.m. But breakfast plonked on
my tray by what looked like a 'female' ex-shot
putter, was black bread, salami and lukewarm
beer. Ugh!

Funniest flight
My Aer Lingus flight blew a tyre on take-off. We
slewed down the runway amidst great alarm.

Most gymnastic free ride

Portuguese youth Daniel Correra Demelo, aged
seventeen, flew 2000 miles across the Atlantic from
the Azores to Bermuda hiding in the nosewheel of
a Venezuelan Airlines Superconstellation. He was
spotted at Bermuda Airport, alive and well, by one
of the ground staff 'clinging to the tricycle undercarriage like a monkey'.

Daniel survived the nine-hour flight because the
plane flew at 8000 feet instead of the usual 18,000
feet altitude. The navigator had reported hearing 'a

After repairs had been done the nervous passengers were shepherded back in, the plane revved its engines and then the pilot came on and said in broadest brogue, 'OK, folks. Let's give her another try.'

Craziest flight
Being in a small plane in bad weather heading for Philadelphia. The formerly laconic pilot began to get more and more worried as he talked on the intercom . . . Eventually he revealed that all the airports on our route were snowbound. The nearest we could land at was an hour away. Someone had to ask the question, 'How much fuel have we got?' The answer: 'Forty-five minutes' worth!'

In the end we were allowed into snowbound Philadelphia – the only plane in that night – no fun, but thank goodness!

---

noise like someone pounding something', but thought it was the door of the undercarriage swinging open.

Most brazen stowaway (1)

It was revealed in October 1984 that a young American boy had spent a whole year flying the world as a stowaway. An example of his coolness under pressure came after a Honolulu flight, where he flew undetected by entering via the crew door then hiding in the lavatory. Challenged by customs staff on arrival in Australia he burst into tears, telling how he had become separated from his mother. The kind, if gullible, customs men took him through to the exit area, and left him there, saying that was where he would be able to meet her.

Most brazen stowaway (2)

Angela Riley, aged twelve, of Ealing, had gone to London Airport with a friend to watch the planes, but when she heard a flight called for Boston and New York she 'just decided to go and see' her sister Wendy in America. Angela inventively walked up to a woman carrying a baby and asked: 'I'm travelling on this plane with my daddy. Would you like me to help you by carrying your little baby?'

The woman fell for the ploy. Freckle-faced Angela then merely flashed the baby's boarding card at the cabin staff, walked boldly on to the plane, and sat down. No hiding in the loo for her. Not until she was halfway across the Atlantic did she admit to being a stowaway. For her cheek, she ended up with a free return flight to New York (at the time worth £315) and a doll presented to her by BOAC.

Longest distance free runabout

Winning this contest by more than a whisker was a cat named Hamlet. He was found alive at Heathrow Airport in April 1984, after flying 625,000 miles in the hold of a jumbo jet. Hamlet, who escaped from his basket on a flight from Canada to London, survived six weeks in the hold. As well as a number of transatlantic crossings, he logged visits to the West Indies and Australia.

The Mile High Club

A stewardess on a Gulf Air jet in September 1976 made an embarrassing discovery. After investigating 'certain noises', she was forced to report to the captain that she had discovered a couple making enthusiastic and blissful love in one of the lavatories. Yes, they had been trying to join the 'Mile High Club'. The captain knew exactly what to do. As the couple strolled smugly back to their places, he announced over the intercom: 'For the man and woman returning to their seats, I must point out that we have been travelling at 5000 feet, and that is not quite a mile high.'

Others, however, *have* been known to join the elite fraternities who have performed a mile (or five miles) high . . .

Naughtiest air hostess

This was undoubtedly Miss Jane Whitehead, aged thirty, of Air New Zealand who, in August 1984, was sacked for molesting male passengers while travelling off-duty on a flight from Auckland to Hawaii. After drinking five glasses of champagne it was alleged that Miss Whitehead offered a glass to a male acquaintance and told him 'let's go down the back'. They then entered a lavatory and made passionate love 30,000 feet above the Pacific. The aerial 'I'm Jane, fly me' session came to an abrupt end, however, when the male friend accidentally caught himself on the 'assistance required' button. Miss Whitehead was then said to have 'annoyed' other passengers by climbing on top of them provocatively, stripping off her dress, and revealing she was no longer wearing any knickers. In the case of the purser she is alleged to have kneed him in the groin, fondled his genitals, and asked him to make mad passionate love to her. The virtually naked hostess ended the flight with her legs wrapped round one of the crew member's necks.

Sir Ranulph Fiennes

History-making round-the-world explorer

Favourite airline
British Airways. They once held up a plane for fifteen minutes because I was late for a lecture in Florida.

Least favourite
Air France. A particular dreadful flight from Italy to Paris last year will long live in my memory.

Favourite air story
My Scottish cousin, *not* inebriated, awoke in mid-flight. Outside it was still and pure white. He thought we'd arrived in Pisa, grabbed his case and headed for the exit. Fortunately the hostess stopped him.

Miss Whitehead said she remembered nothing. Her lawyer said the champagne had unfortunately reacted rather strongly with some sleeping pills Miss Whitehead had taken (I think I'd like some of those – Ed.). An out-of-court settlement was reached with Air New Zealand after Miss Whitehead claimed unfair dismissal. (Yes, you'd have thought they'd have used her in the next advertising campaign instead!)

Most public enrolment in the five mile high club

He sat in seat 25A. A married woman, she sat in seat 19A. The attraction between them was instant. She left 19A to join him beside 25A. And then things on BOAC VC-10 Flight 591 from New York to Honolulu got a little heated.

Another couple behind complained to the chief steward of the 'profane language, lewd talk and noises' coming from seat 25A. They were molesting each other, they said. Mrs 19A (now sharing 25A) became irate and demanded to see the captain.

He remonstrated with Mr 25A and Mrs 19A (now stretching across 25A and 25B): 'Will you kindly control your actions. They are causing a lot of inconvenience to other passengers.' (Translated in a later report to: 'Please fasten your chastity belts.')

The result was chaos, according to a report in the BOAC magazine *Horizon*.

The captain told Mrs 19A (25A and 25B) to return to seat 19A. Mrs 19A (25A and 25B) threatened to kill him.

Finally she complied, taking Mr 25A with her, but only to carry on where they left off on seat 19A, with lovemaking in full view of the chief steward and other passengers.

All was soon quiet, however. After their exertions, Mrs 19A and Mr 25A, now united in seat 19A, both fell asleep. The captain said in his report: 'I knew they just needed to get if off and then would not be of any more inconvenience to other passengers.'

Most celebrated case of love at first flight

This happened to the late critic Mr Kenneth Tynan, and will be forever associated with him as will the four-letter word which he was the first to use on BBC Television. Unlike most members of the Mile High Club, who inevitably have other partners to go home to, Mr Tynan not only talked about it afterwards but wrote about it for *Punch*.

The story went like this. Mr Tynan had, in 1958, just been appointed drama critic of the *New Yorker* and was returning to London in a state of exultation and regretting he had no one to share his rush of blood to the extremities. Aha! Relief was at hand. He was 'placed alongside a pretty dark-haired girl, guessably in her mid-twenties'. They didn't talk. She covered herself with a blanket and settled down for the night.

Said Tynan, 'I had half a bottle of champagne inside me, and it occurred to me that I would very much like to make love to her.' Thus he removed the chair arm that lay between them, threw over a couple of blankets and started to let his hand creep under her skirt, no doubt muttering sweet nothings like 'Oh, Calcutta!' Tynan explained how he 'came up against the armadillo-like casing of a girdle'. Acknowledging defeat, he withdrew his hand.

Ah yes, but suddenly the girl sat bolt upright, seized her handbag, and sprang to her feet. She was obviously going to report the matter. Tynan could see the headlines: 'Girl goosed over Gander.' But no! She was merely removing her girdle, placing it in her handbag, to enable Tynan 'by moving against her in what is known as the spoon position, to achieve an enchanting slow-motion climax'.

Tynan then broke all love at first-flight convention and spoke to her. He even asked her out for dinner. This was, of course, quite over the top. The 'still-knickerless hypocrite' cooled his aeronautical ardour by insisting this would be most improper. 'My parents don't like me to go out with people I haven't been introduced to,' she replied coolly.

Smoothest and most sophisticated chat-up technique

Leading Lothario of the airliner aisles, Mr John Coghlan, former drummer with Status Quo, wins this accolade by a (vertical) mile with this description from the *Star* in January 1986 of how he joined the Five Mile High Club on a jumbo jet to Australia:

'We were somewhere over the Indian Ocean and everyone was settling down to sleep upstairs in the first-class lounge. One of the hostesses came round to tuck me in. I was sitting alone, drinking champagne.

'I persuaded her to sit down and have a sip. *As soon as she did I knew something was on.*' Or off, as the case may be.

Pray let Mr Coghlan continue: 'I had a blanket over me, and she soon disappeared under it.' (She was probably cold, or looking for another bottle of champagne – Ed.) 'Then I whispered, 'Go to the

127

washroom!' She straightened herself up and wandered off.' (Well wouldn't you if anyone talked to you like that – Ed.)

'After a minute I followed her to the washroom ... I tried the wrong one first ... there was only an old dear in it who was most annoyed about my persistent knocking.' (So would I have been. 'This

---

Mike Smith

TV presenter and pop pundit

Favourite airline
Brymon Airways (London to Plymouth). They still have barley sugar – and you often end up in Newquay.

Least favourite
Sabena. The steward stopped my girlfriend from painting her nails – he said it was dangerous. Yet they still allow smoking on aircraft!

Most unusual story
A friend was travelling as a courier to New York. The valuable documents he wasn't supposed to let out of his hands got left in the departure lounge. Undeterred, he got the jumbo turned back just as it was approaching take-off.

Craziest flight
Once, on a journey from Miami to London, the cabin crew let me sleep *all* the way. No stupid

is an airliner, not a knocking shop' – Ed.)

'Our bit of fun lasted about twenty minutes, which at average jumbo jet speed means the nookie covered about 200 miles.'

(That's a man for you, always bragging about the length of his nookie – Ed.'s wife.)

announcements. No banging into me with the duty-free trolley. No waking me up to ask if I wanted a drink. They just let me sleep. Amazing!

The most mind-boggling display of sensual opulence ever assembled in a flying machine

This is not my own, but *Newsweek*'s description of Mr Hugh Hefner's aerial plaything, the specially converted and liveried DC–9 known as 'the Big Bunny' he bought in 1969 for some $5,300,000.

Outside, the plane was painted macho stud-black, to make it resemble a cigarette or contraceptive packet.

Inside a further $500,000 was spent on turning Big Bunny into a flying Versailles. Hefner's personal quarters near the tail included a 6' x 8' elliptical bed upholstered in black Himalayan goat-skin, covered with white silk sheets and a Tasmanian opossum pelt bedspread. A special belt was fitted across the bed so that Mr Hefner and his companion of the hour could stay horizontal during take-off and landing.

The stewardesses, designated 'Jet Bunnies', were selected from the best of the Playboy girls and equipped with eyecatching $500 'uniforms' of wet-look black nylon mini skirts, thigh-length boots and white silk scarves, emblazoned with little 'wings' as well as the Playboy logo. Nevertheless, for all its long-ride capabilities, Big Bunny was mostly used by Mr Hefner for a 'bus-stop' hop between Chicago and Los Angeles.

Worst side-effects of in-flight gymnastics

In November 1978 100 planes of the Japanese airline JAL were grounded because too many passengers had being trying to join the Five Mile High

Club. The problem was the sleeper service that the airline introduced on long-distance flights. Hostesses were so distressed by naked forms and 'lewd' behaviour, they went on strike for twenty-four hours as a protest, grounding the entire JAL fleet. Urging an end to the new service on 'moral grounds', stewardesses told how they found particularly distressing the number of male passengers who showed themselves stripped down and ready for action when they pulled back curtains and tried to offer drinks.

Julie Walters

Academy-award-nominated actress

Favourite airline
Qantas. They know how to do it, and look as if they enjoy doing it – like good lovers.

Least favourite
British West Indies! They are filled with loathing for their passengers. Serve food as if they wished it was poison, and it tastes as if it is!

Craziest experience
On a long flight I sat next to a really rude man. We got into a discussion about feminism – I got upset with him and told him he treated his wife badly (she was the other side of him). He hadn't spoken to her since the flight started. Just before we landed I discovered she was dead! She'd had a very quiet heart attack during the journey – and he still treated her badly!

The world's sexiest airline

If a 'fly and tell' memoir by the appropriately named Mr Roy Bedson, a pilot, is to be believed, this accolade should go to Regent Airlines, who run a fleet of luxury-fitted 727s primarily for pop and film stars. According to Mr B., the planes are fitted with bar, bathroom, and four compartments which serve as 'private bedrooms' when the seats are folded down. These were the scene of much action, he told the *Sun*. The crew were told to turn a blind eye, except for the 'good-looking stewardesses who were only too willing to join in the fun'.

Mr Bedson had clearly not turned a blind eye, regaling his readers with lurid accounts of the frolics of the famous aboard what was dubbed 'The Love Plane'. There was, for example:

Barry Manilow who had a face like a thunderstorm until a severe bout of turbulence providently thrust stunning Morgan Fairchild on to his lap (it's a wonder he wasn't crushed to death).

Rod Stewart (who else?) who allegedly pulled Christie Brinkley (in her pre-Joel days) away from the attentions of a boring businessman. He dragged her, in fact, right back to one of those private compartments Mr Bedson was so keen to write about. 'The laughing and giggling from behind the curtains told everybody on the plane that they had become good friends.' (Obviously they were playing Trivial Pursuit.) The pair were not seen again, reported Mr B., until they emerged together from the love plane's bathroom with Cheshire cat grins on their faces.

Lee Majors. A sad story this. According to Mr B., the million-dollar man invited two tipsy girls back to his 'private compartment' for a game of 'spin the bottle'. This required the loser of each spin to remove an article of clothing. The problem was, Mr Majors was a bad loser, being quite keen for the girls to take their clothes off, but reluctant to take off his own. When the two girls tried to undress him forcibly, he called the chief stewardess and had them removed (the two girls, not his clothes).

Biggest mile-high spoilsports

Having joined the illustrious club themselves, according to their ex-drummer John Coghlan, the rock group Status Quo used to put on the meanest of shows during long flights. He told the *Star:* 'We would wait until the lights had gone out then start creeping about the plane looking for people at it under the blankets. When we found someone we'd all jump on them.' (Watch it, this is a family book – Ed.)

Most decadent private jet

This was undoubtedly the Rolling Stones DC-7, which ferried them across America on their tours of the early 1970s, at least according to revered US author Truman Capote, who was allowed the privilege of jetting about with the group and their entourage.

In the recent book *Conversations With Capote* (Laurence Grobel, Hutchinson, 1985) Mr C. told how he found all the Rolling Stones 'quite mad'. Travelling with them was 'quite astonishing', he said.

'There was this drink that they all drank called Tequila Sunrise. And this little girl who was supposed to be the stewardess would pass down the aisle with this plate of every kind of pill that you can imagine. Then up at the front of the plane was this very well-known man who made documentary films making pornographic movies of different people, including the Rolling Stones, having sex with some total stranger they had picked up in the town we'd just been in.'

Added Capote with a twinkle in his eye: 'It was like being in a blue movie for two solid weeks.'

Mr Capote had waxed lyrical about a Rolling Stones plane journey before, in April 1973, when he produced an exclusive piece for the underground magazine *Rolling Stone* (no relation). The highlight of his piece was the description of how a youngster who wanted to write an article for her school magazine was taken aboard the plane by a young doctor known for his penchant for young girls. They then made love for the cameras under a set of arc lights in the plane's rear 'in every conceivable position'. Capote told her: 'Well you came to get a story for your high-school newspaper, and you've certainly been given one.'

Most famous sex bomb to join the mile high club

In an interview with the *Sun* in November 1985, Patrick Curtis, the film producer formerly married to Raquel Welch told in Technicolor detail how the screen sex goddess had ordered him to follow her into the lavatory during an Alitalia flight to Rome. 'We joined the Mile High Club at 500 miles an hour. It was ecstatic. We hit cloud nine,' the paper quoted him as saying. Mr Curtis said that when Raquel made her come hither move he had not realized how near to landing they were.

'Suddenly lights started flashing – "Fasten your

seat belts, extinguish cigarettes." And everyone could see our seats were empty. That made it even more exciting. Raquel loved it – we both did.' Mr Curtis said what they enjoyed most was 'the race against time'.

'The plane hit an air pocket and our passion exploded just as we touched down,' he said. 'Then we came out in tandem and the whole plane, being

---

Rula Lenska

Stage and TV actress

Favourite airline
British Airways, simply because they are always especially nice to us and wonderful with children, and Ansett – Australia's interstate airline – for the same reason.

Least favourite
Pan Am – when we flew with our children the staff seemed impatient and unwilling to help in any way.

Most memorable flight
The first time I flew – and I had put it off through terror for many years – I was looking out of the window (two Mogadons and several drinks inside of me) when, as I now realize is usual just prior to take-off, the wing flaps were lowered. In total panic I rang for the stewardess shouting at the top of my voice, 'We can't take off, the wing has just broken in half.'

Italian, burst into applause. I being Irish, took a bow,' he added with pride. Commented the *Sun*, without apparently noticing the pun: 'That was just one of the joyrides Mr Curtis found himself on during eight years of marriage to the amazing Miss Welch . . .'

Most discreet entry into the mile high club

In her book *The Stewardesses* (Sphere, 1973), former hostess Penny Sutton told of a certain type of jet where the lavatories are side by side and it is a little-known fact that the wall between them is detachable.

Says Penny: 'It is therefore possible to trot off individually without provoking suspicion and join up later – if that is the right expression – after a little basic carpentry.'

AUTHOR'S NOTE: *Watch this one.* Make sure it is the object of your desires in the adjacent loo and you do *not* surprise a Turkish heavyweight wrestler with his trousers down. You may have to pay the penalty!

The most passionate post-flight embrace

It was not quite love at a great height, but a couple go into the record books (well, this one at least) for making love twelve minutes after a flight arrival, yes, on the moving walkway of Heathrow Airport's Terminal Three.

The young man had just arrived from New York one day in October 1981, and had been met by a pretty blonde. First they kissed . . . then they

embraced . . . then . . . it was obvious they had come closer still. Some passengers averted their eyes. Some averted their children's eyes. Some averted their wives' eyes. Some averted their husbands' eyes. But most stood and watched, transfixed by the post-flight entertainment.

There was a brief and unfortunate interruption to the show as the couple had to hop from one section of the walkway to another. But those who had stayed for the moving floor show were rewarded when they took up, just as before.

Said stewardess Jenny Rees, who said she saw 'everything' (may Aer Lingus preserve us): 'I couldn't believe my eyes. They only had a short trip on the walkways, but it was action-packed. I suppose there had to be something after the Mile High Club!'

The couple were not available for interview afterwards. An airport official pointed out that they had moved on to (the moving promenades of?) Paris. He said, 'It was obvious. They just got carried away . . .' Yes, the earth must have moved for both of them.

Plane Crazy

There was the inventor who begged to be let out of the Britannia aircraft at 15,000 feet to test the new parachute he had just designed . . .

The elderly couple halfway to Australia who tried to get out 'because we've just remembered we left the gas on' . . .

And the Concorde passenger who spurned the Lobster Newburg and Millionaire's Salad, pulled out a paper bag and asked, 'Can you warm up this Big Mac?'

Like I have said. It's a *Plane Crazy* world . . .

Most oblivious first flyer

A BEA Vanguard airliner was about to take off from Amsterdam in November 1968, when the captain on the flight deck saw a red warning light. The light indicated an emergency hatch had been opened so he asked cabin staff to investigate. They were astonished to see seventy-year-old Johan Patist, from Utrecht, Holland, sitting by the open hatch and waving cheerfully to relatives who had come to see him off on a trip to visit his daughter in New Zealand.

Mr Patist explained it was his first flight. When he got on he was delighted to see his family waving from the visitor's roof. He wanted to open a window

Jon Pertwee

Actor and former 'Doctor Who'

Favourite airline
Cathay Pacific. Because of the superb-looking air
hostesses, the superlative food and the general
cleanliness of the aircraft. To have travelled some
fourteen hours in any airplane and still be relaxed
at the end of it, must make it good.

Least favourite
Air Maroc. The service was appalling. When we
rang the bell nothing happened as they were busy
playing obscure Arabic board games. It would seem
that service to the passengers was an intrusion
into their privacy.

Most bizarre experience
When flying Air Kenya from Nairobi to Mombasa,
I was entering the loo when a large chieftain shot
in behind me and slammed the door. I was
concerned as to his purpose and attempted to get
past his immense bulk and out again to safety, but
he wouldn't open the door. When I querulously

and wave back, so he pulled a red handle above his
head, stuck out a hand and waved. The captain was
not amused. He ordered the eighty passengers back
into the airport lounge while the hatch was
resealed.

asked him why not, by now utterly alarmed, he said his wife was after him and that was the only haven of refuge he could think of!

Most surprising last-minute arrival

Executive Travel magazine told how the passengers were belted in, the plane was all ready to leave, and the cabin staff had taken up their take-off positions when there was a frantic hammering on the fuselage of the Bangladeshi aircraft. The crew at first ignored the attempted intrusion – but then relented. Wisely as it turned out. It was the pilot trying to board the plane.

The only shuttle halted by two rashers of streaky bacon

When purser Ted Payne refused to promise Captain R. F. Cooper his breakfast at the scheduled time while bound from Heathrow to Glasgow in April 1981, Captain Cooper, who was taxiing for take-off, turned the plane round, telling astonished passengers: 'This is the captain. There has been a disagreement with a member of the cabin crew. In the interests of safety we are returning to the loading bay.'

Startled Ted was then told to disembark and another purser, who was prepared to serve the captain with his sausages, mushrooms and bacon at the appointed time was taken aboard. Passengers, also awaiting their streaky bacon, were delayed twenty minutes by the 'no fry, no fly' row.

A friend of the purser said, 'Ted offered to serve the meal either before or after he collected the fares and sold the walk-on tickets. But the captain wouldn't have it. He wanted his breakfast on the dot.'

... and the only plane hit by an egg

A light plane flying at more than 100 m.p.h. at White Waltham, Berks, was hit by an unusual flying object ... an egg. Unfried, of course – it had been laid by a bird in mid-flight. The pilot, ex-Wing Commander V.C. Varose said, 'It was a million to one chance.' Mr John Yealland, curator of birds at

London Zoo said, 'I have never heard before of a bird laying an egg in flight.'

Most amazing bird strike

Among many birds of prey attempting to take a chunk out of the flight crew stories I have read, one (*Great Travelling Disasters*, by Hugh Vickers and Caroline McCullough, Papermac, 1984) concerned a

Robin Knox-Johnston

Single-handed, round-the-world record-breaking yachtsman

Best airline
British Airways, for two reasons. First because I feel safer in their hands; second because they had the intelligence to sponsor me.

Worst airline
The Red Devils (who run an Islander). All the time I was with them, I was horribly conscious of the door missing, and the fact that they were going to throw me out of the gap any minute. Only with them have I failed to arrive at my destination in the aircraft I commenced the journey!

Most unusual flight
Once we got lost over Devon, and eventually strayed into an RAF controlled zone. They were not at all pleased. But we were delighted as it told us where we were!

plane 'eaten by a vulture' during a flight in Botswana. The hungry feathered enemy was said to have chomped merrily away in mid-flight at one of the wings and then appeared in the cockpit fixing its beady eye carnivorously on the pilot, forcing the plane to crash-land.

Believe that or not, the most amazing (and very first) bird strike officially documented took place in 1911 during the Paris-Madrid air race, when over the plain of Somosierra, pioneer aviator Eugene Gilbert was attacked by an (extremely hungry) flight of eagles. He was carrying just the right equipment in case eagles dared, of course, and, the cockpit being somewhat more open-plan in those days than in the reign of the 747s, he despatched the giant birds of prey with a number of deadly shots from his revolver.

Most unusual landing hazard

The pilot of a Sabena airliner had an unusual hazard to contend with as he came in to land at Paris in December 1965 – a plague of frogs. He reported 'thousands' of the frogs invaded the flight deck and leaped around him as he touched down safely. An airline spokesman said luckily the flight was only a short 'hop'.

Worst-ever hijacker

A Briton expelled from Germany burst into the cockpit of a Lufthansa plane in March 1985 demanding: 'Take me to Heathrow.' For once the captain was happy to oblige. That was where they were going anyway. On landing in London fifteen minutes later the slapstick hijacker changed his tack ... 'We're going to Honolulu,' he told his by now weary captives. The plane was surrounded by armed police, but the hijacker was quickly forced to surrender when he responded to a call to come to the plane's door to negotiate. 'You don't expect me to fall for a trick like that,' said the hijacker. He then promptly appeared at the plane's door and was seized.

Most unusual case of 'buzzing' in flight

An airliner flying from Amsterdam to Paris suddenly became the centre of a pitched battle between the captain, crew, and passengers and an unlikely band of 'hijackers': a swarm of thousands of bees. Many of the passengers were stung, and the bees were in turn swatted and killed. The anti-social insects – four million of them – had been packed in 150 crates in the cargo hold for distribution to English beekeepers. They did not seem to have enjoyed their flight. When the plane landed, porters and officials winged it for cover but they too were attacked and stung. Half an hour later outside the freight shed thousands were still swarming, looping and stinging.

Most relieved passengers

These, according to Mr Dougal (Peter) Butler in his book *Moon the Loon* (Star, 1981), were the poor souls who accompanied his boss, the late drummer with The Who, on a flight from Los Angeles to London. According to Mr Butler, 'Keith didn't need an aircraft to fly – he was already higher than Saturn, fuelled by a handful of valium and three vodkas and tonics.'

'Sure enough,' said our witness, 'once we are in the plane, Moonie heaves into the champagne and orange and after two hours is uncontrollable.'

His subsequent behaviour included distributing his meal in equal measures over the rest of the passengers, trying to get into the cockpit to give directions to the pilot, then springing up suddenly

---

Ernie Wise

Leading comedian and playwright

Favourite airline
Air New Zealand, because of the superb cabin and bar service.

Least favourite
Air Canada. I did not like the cabin service, I'm afraid – and Qantas. The first time I flew to Australia in a Constellation we were stuck on Canton Island for twelve hours in a heat of 104 degrees.

Funniest flight
We were invited into the cockpit. The pilot said we would be in Tenerife in half an hour. We said, 'But we are going to Las Palmas!' The pilot replied, 'Whoops, sorry, I forgot!' and turned the plane round towards Las Palmas!

Most unusual experience
Years ago I stayed in theatrical digs in Chiswick. Living there was a young boy of about fourteen

'and shouting 'YAHAAAAAAAAAAA!!!!' so loud that the tailplane nearly drops off'.

Mr Moon then apparently rendered the public-address system useless by blaring out the Lone Ranger theme from his stereo ghetto-blasters. Just before landing he switched tapes and stood to atten-tion in the aisle, his trousers round his ankles, with

who was mad about aeroplanes. Twenty years later I flew to Malta and guess who was the pilot – yes, the young boy from those Chiswick digs!

his cassette machine blasting out 'Land of Hope and Glory'.

Said Mr Butler: 'Stone me if this last effort doesn't receive thunderous applause from all our fellow passengers.' He added: 'Though not for any sense of patriotism, it is on account of the fact that everyone is so relieved that we have landed safe and sound despite having such a lunatic on board.'

Highest altitude recorded in a deckchair

Astonished pilots coming in to land at Long Beach Airport, California, in December 1982, radioed the control tower to report a bizarre sight bobbing in the clouds three miles high – Larry Walters, aged thirty-three, flying high in a lawnchair.

As a lark reclining Larry had tied forty-two gas-filled weather balloons to his chair. He expected to hover just a couple of hundred feet high, but instead soared towards the stratosphere. At 16,000 feet he decided he had gone high enough, and managed to get himself back down to earth by shooting some of the balloons with an air pistol.

There was another shock for Larry when he made it back to terra firma – a £2500 fine for flying without a licence. He said, 'I'm innocent. I never meant to fly so high.'

Most successful impromptu in-flight repairs

In July 1966 9000 feet over Belgrade, Montana, a rodeo rider averted disaster when he hung out of an airplane and kicked the jammed landing gear into

place. The feat was repeated in August 1981 by
stuntman Roland Schneider, appropriately enough
over John Wayne Airport south of Los Angeles.

Most unusual aircraft ejection seats

Four passengers, three men and a woman, were
'ejected' from their lavatory seats on a jumbo jet

General Alexander Haig

*Former US Secretary of State and NATO Supreme
Allied Commander, Europe*

General Haig made the following remarks, he
recalled to me, when accepting the presidential
nomination in January 1980 at the Alfalfa Club.
This is a Washington DC male social organization
which meets annually in fun to nominate in jest a
candidate for US president. General Haig was the
candidate in 1980, six months after returning from
active duty military service as Supreme Allied
Commander, Europe:

'One of the reasons I want to be President is to
ride on Air Force One again. I am tired of using
commuter planes. That's how candidates spend all
their time, you know – on commuter airlines. I
flew in on one. Maybe you heard of it – Air
Gaithersburg. It's the first time I've ever been on
a plane that stops for red lights. Thirty minutes
after departure time, I glanced out the window
and I said to the stewardess, "Look at that. Those
people down there look like ants." She said,
"General, they are ants, we haven't left yet." '

150

flight from New York to London in May 1974.

A sudden surge of air turbulence, which dipped the tail of the aircraft sharply, was blamed for the unexpected in-flight take-off. All four suffered back injuries, said the airline, though none needed hospital treatment.

Most disastrous visit to the lavatory

In October 1970 Mr F. Jacinski, a sixty-year-old Pole, decided to go to the washroom while over the Irish Sea on a BAC One-Eleven en route from Dublin to London. Unfortunately he chose the wrong door. This one led out of the aircraft.

Seeing a red warning light come on which indicated a door had been opened, the pilot made an emergency landing at Manchester Ringway. On landing Mr Jacinski, who had been trapped between the inner and the outer pressurized door, fell out of the plane on to the tarmac. (It could have been worse, at least he didn't fall out into the Irish Sea.) He was all right though, and to the immense relief of Mr Jacinski and everyone else, having been shown the washroom in the airport terminal, he went on to complete his journey.

Most embarrassing lost luggage

There was a frantic search when a case was lost on a Concorde flight. Its owner: the operations and maintenance planning manager of British Airways.

Cheekiest airport thief

Thefts from air freight and luggage became so prevalent at London Airport that for a time it became known as 'Thiefrow'. Things have changed since, of course. But a favourite story is told there of the loader who tried to rifle through a mailbag and became locked in the plane's cargo hold. He emerged at Glasgow when the cargo doors were opened with a well-rehearsed look of indignation saying: 'I'm going to want double the overtime for this trip.'

Eamonn Andrews

Leading TV presenter

Best airline
Florida Air Lines, the only airline in the world ever to give me a free trip. It broke my heart to note they went bankrupt shortly afterwards!

Worst airlines
All the other airlines who never did give me a free trip, and, in particular, the internal American airline whose hostess said 'Hi' as I entered the plane and then proceeded to treat me like a piece of furniture thereafter. 'Hi' thereafter joined that American list of mine that includes 'Have a good day'.

Craziest flight
An ex-American flyer came to live in Shannon with a tiny monoplane he'd flown all the way from Italy, hop by hop, and known as the Flying Flea. As a publicity stunt for a radio show I was doing in Dublin at the time, he agreed to fly me from Shannon to Dublin with some records I'd had

Worst-dressed passenger

This honour undoubtedly belongs to the forty-seven-year-old Australian who, in December 1985, ran wild aboard a Qantas flight dressed only in a cardigan. It was back to front (the cardigan, not the Qantas flight). Passengers and cabin staff became a little edgy when the semi-naked man then tried to

flown over from New York. We buzzed up through the Irish Midlands happily, a beautiful day, with me sitting directly behind him. I shouted at him if it was all right to smoke.

'Just a moment,' he yelled back. To my terror, he zoomed straight down, skimming the hedges, landed in a field, opened the door, invited me out and said, 'Yeah, now you may smoke!'

open the plane doors, shouting: 'I'm going to get off this bus.'

Most unsuccessful airline promotion

An American airline decided to try and improve its passenger figures by encouraging wives to travel with their husbands on business trips. So its computer was asked to provide a list of the wives who recently accompanied their menfolk on flights, and each one was mailed a special offer of discount flights.

They had plenty of replies. Unfortunately most of them were from wives demanding: 'Who was the woman with my husband on his last business trip? It certainly wasn't me.'

Plane Crazy!!!

On the following pages are details of Arrow books that will be of interest.

A LITTLE ZIT ON THE SIDE

Jasper Carrott

He's been a delivery boy (the terror of Solihull), a toothpaste salesman (for four hours), a folkie (repertoire – two songs) – and the most unlikely and original comic superstar for years.

Now Jasper Carrott reveals more of the outrageous talent that has taken him from the Boggery to a series of one-man shows that won him I T V's Personality of the Year Award.

Discover the do-it-yourself man, how to become star of Top of the Pops and the Carrott guide to dog-training. Relive the simple pleasures of The Magic Roundabout, Funky Moped and the Mole.

THE UNLUCKIEST MAN IN THE WORLD
and similar disasters

Mike Harding

Born in the picturesque spa of Lower Crumpsall, he spent his early years in the brooding shadow of a cream cracker factory. At the age of seventeen he bought a set of Mongolian bagpipes and joined a rock and roll band. Much of his manhood has been spent waiting for a girl wearing red feathers and a hulu skirt to come into his life. He is the incorrigible, irrepressible and slightly mad Mike Harding.

The Unluckiest Man in the World takes us into the world of Mike Harding with an inimitable collection of happy, sad, ridiculous, profound and simply hilarious songs, poems and stories.

GULLIBLE'S TRAVELS

Billy Connolly

He has travelled from the majestic deserts of Doha (twin town of Drumchapel in Scotland) and the teeming markets of Bletchley to the splendour of the Sydney surf and the exotic decadence of the Crawley Leisure Centre.

And here it is — a unique guide to the world, travel, life, death and camel-smells, as seen through the eyes of

'the gangling Glaswegian doyen of bad taste' *Daily Telegraph*

'the man who makes Bette Midler look like Jess Conrad' *The Stage*

'one of the most outrageous Scotsmen ever to have vaulted Hadrian's Wall' *Daily Express*

'the laughing laureate of the loo' *The Times*

the inimitable (thank God) BILLY CONNOLLY

Compiled by Duncan Campbell

Illustrated by Steve Bell

THE ART OF COARSE SEX

Michael Green

Undaunted by the advice of romantic novelists, sex therapists or agony aunts, Michael Green thrusts onwards into the hitherto virgin territory of THE ART OF COARSE SEX. The dismal difficulties of outdoor sex, the ghastly complexities and consequences of furtive affairs, the mysteries of sexual attraction – all this and more is ruthlessly, wickedly and hilariously exposed as Michael Green gets to the bottom of Man's oldest obsession.

THE DIETER'S GUIDE TO WEIGHT LOSS DURING SEX

Richard Smith

Tired? Listless? Overweight? Open this book at any page and discover everything you wanted to know about sex, food and dieting but never dreamt of asking.

Activity	Calories burned
REMOVING CLOTHES	
With partner's consent	12
Without partner's consent	187
Unhooking bra	
Using two calm hands	7
Using one trembling hand	96
EMBARRASSMENT	
Large juice stain on shorts	10
ORGASM	
Real	27
Faked	160

(Continued on page 81)